THE BEST OF
SAMAITHU PAAR

S. Meenakshi Ammal

(1906-1962)

THE BEST OF
SAMAITHU PAAR

The Classic Guide to Tamil Cuisine

S. MEENAKSHI AMMAL

Food Photographs by Ashish Chawla

VIKING

VIKING

Penguin Books India (P) Ltd., 11 Community Centre, Panchsheel Park, New Delhi 110017, India

Penguin Books Ltd., 80 Strand, London, WC2R 0RL

Penguin Putnam Inc., 375 Hudson Street, New York, NY 10014, USA

Penguin Books Australia Ltd., Ringwood, Victoria, Australia

Penguin Books Canada Ltd., 10 Alcorn Avenue, Suite 300, Toronto, Ontario, M4V 3B2, Canada

Penguin Books (NZ) Ltd., Cnr Rosedale & Airborne Roads, Albany, Auckland, New Zealand

First published in VIKING by Penguin Books India 2001
Text copyright © S. Meenakshi Ammal Publications 2001
Photographs copyright © Penguin Books India 2001

10 9 8 7 6 5 4 3 2 1

Inserts: Food prepared and photographed at Dakshin, Marriott WelcomHotel, Delhi
Cover: Photographed at Kandahar, The Oberoi, Delhi. Copyright © DK Picture Library

Printed at Thomson Press, Noida

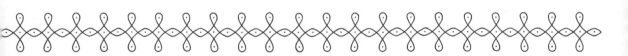

CONTENTS

Tiffin

Rice Pongal	51
Sweet Pongal	52
Broken Wheat Pongal	53
Idli (with par-boiled rice)	54
Idli (with raw rice)	56
Semolina Idli	57
Dosai	58
Wheat Dosai	60
Semolina Dosai	61
Wheat Flour Jaggery Dosai	62
Oothappam	65
Adai	66
Jaggery Adai	68
Pesarat	69
Poori	70
Semolina Uppuma	71
Rice Uppuma	72
Broken Wheat Uppuma	73
Vermicelli Uppuma	74
Tamarind Flavoured Beaten Rice Flakes	75
Semia Bahala Bath	76
Vadai	77
Curd Vadai	78
Kara Vadai	79
Mysore Bonda	80
Potato Bonda	83
Bajji	84

Savouries

Murukku	87
Black Gram Dhal Thenkuzhal	88
Ribbon Thenkuzhal	89
Omappodi	90
Kara Boondhi	91
Mixture	92

Sweets

Vermicelli Payasam	95
Green Gram Dhal Payasam	96
Sago Payasam	97

PREFACE

It has been said, if all the cookbooks ever published were lined up, they would stretch all the way to the moon. This is a reflection of the immense popularity of this genre today. However, this was not so back in the fifties in India when my mother S. Meenakshi Ammal first published *Samaithu Paar*. Traditionally, cooking skills were handed down from one generation to the next by word of mouth and referring to a cookery book would probably have been considered sacrilegious. Born into a traditional Tamilian family, this was the environment in which the author grew up and lived. Considered an expert cook in her family, she was constantly besieged with requests for recipes by her relatives. Having to write out the same recipes endlessly made her think of writing a book. But her idea met with resistance. Many were quick to discourage. The only encouragement came from her uncle, Shri K. V. Krishnaswami Iyer, a leading advocate, ex-president of The Music Academy, Chennai, and considered to be the father of the Library Movement in Tamilnadu. With his support, Meenakshi Ammal published the first volume of *Samaithu Paar* in Tamil in 1951. The simple style of writing, the easy-to-follow directions and the attention to the smallest of details found immense favour with the public. The second and third volumes were published in quick succession. Today, all three volumes have been translated into English and the first volume has also been translated into Hindi, Telugu, Malayalam and Kannada, running into many editions. The continued popularity of *Samaithu Paar* is borne out by its presence on the many lists (available on the Internet) of things to pack for students travelling to the US. It would not be an exaggeration then to say that the book has certainly 'gone places'. Perhaps the ultimate tribute to Meenakshi Ammal came when the ultra-modern lifestyle magazine, *Cosmopolitan*, crowned *Samaithu Paar* the best in its category of classic cookbooks.

In the fifty years since the first volume was published, cooking has undergone many changes, and these changes have been incorporated into *Samaithu Paar*. For example, revisions have been made in the measurement of ingredients, from the original ollocks to grams to the now popular cups. Likewise, references to traditional utensils and kitchen appliances have also been modified. What has not changed is the basic recipes themselves. And, like in the original volume, one caveat remains: this book, as any other of its kind, can only be a guide. Perfection can be achieved only after attempting each recipe a few times. Also, individual tastes differ and need to be factored in when preparing any dish.

In this, the golden jubilee year of *Samaithu Paar*, I take great pride in the fact that Penguin is bringing out this well-designed, definitive edition of the original, choosing the most-loved recipes and making them available to a much wider audience. I hope you, the reader, will enjoy trying out the various recipes as much as we did putting them together.

Chennai   P. S. SANKARAN
November 2001

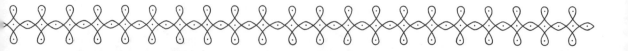

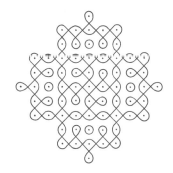

SAMBAR & RASAM

SAMBAR

A variety of vegetables—drumstick, lady's finger, onion, brinjal, pumpkin, Bangalore brinjal, carrot, French beans, runner beans, etc.,—can be used to prepare sambar. Select any one vegetable. Cut into medium size bits and wash. Vegetables like onion, brinjal, lady's finger, French beans, runner beans and cluster beans can also be fried a little before adding. Amaranth stems, radish, runner beans, cluster beans or pumpkin may be cooked separately with just enough salt and then added.

Soak the tamarind in 1 cup water for 20 minutes. Squeeze it out, adding water little by little to prepare 1 cup of juice.

Choose a heavy vessel, e.g., stoneware, with a very narrow mouth. Wash the dhal. Clean and remove stones, if any. (If the dhal is cleanly husked, it need not be washed.) Boil 1-1 1/4 cups of water. Add the dhal, turmeric powder and 1 tsp oil. Cover with a shallow lid, filled with water. (A cup of water may also be placed on the lid.) Add this water to the dhal, if needed, while the dhal is cooking. Cook till very soft. (Some dhals do not cook soon. If so, add a pinch of baking soda. If baking soda is added, do not use turmeric powder, as the colour of the dhal will be spoilt.) Remove from fire and mash the cooked dhal. Keep aside.

Heat a vessel. Pour in the remaining oil. Pinch red chillies into halves. Slit green chillies. Fry the pinched

Ingredients

Vegetable 1/4-1/2 kg
New tamarind A lump the size of a small lime
Red gram dhal 2/3 cup
Turmeric powder 1/2 tsp
Gingelly oil 3 tsp
Dry red chillies 10 (Medium) or 6 (Large)
Green chillies 2
Mustard seeds 1/2 tsp
Fenugreek seeds 1/2 tsp
Asafoetida powder A pinch or to taste
Curry leaves (Chopped) 3 tbsp
Salt 1 tsp
Rice flour 1/2 tsp
Coriander leaves (Chopped) 3 tbsp

To serve 4 persons

Photograph on p. 9

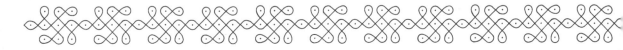

red chillies, mustard, fenugreek seeds and asafoetida to a dark brown colour (without blackening it). Add green chillies. Pinch curry leaves and fry for a few moments. Add the tamarind juice to the seasonings with salt. Add the cut and washed vegetable.

When the vegetable is cooked in the tamarind juice, add the mashed dhal. Allow it to boil well. Mix the rice flour in water. Add and stir well. Bring to boil once more. Boil for a few minutes. Remove from fire. Garnish with coriander leaves and a few curry leaves.

Note:
Asafoetida water may be used in the place of asafoetida powder. If using asafoetida water, add to the sambar when boiling.

To prepare thicker sambar, increase the quantity of dhal.

The dhal can be cooked in a pressure cooker as well.

BUTTERMILK SAMBAR

(MOAR SAMBAR)

A variety of vegetables can be used in the preparation of this dish. It is most commonly made with drumstick, brinjal or lady's finger. Alternatively, potatoes, Bangalore brinjal or ash gourd may also be used. Choose any one vegetable. Wash and cut the vegetable. Cook the vegetable with salt, till soft, in water. Drain out excess water. Keep aside. If using brinjal or lady's finger, do not cook in water. Fry them a little with salt before adding.

Cook the dhal till soft. (See Sambar recipe on p. 3.) Heat the oil in a heavy, e.g., stoneware, vessel. Fry mustard and fenugreek seeds and pinched red chillies to a reddish brown colour. Add slit green chillies and fry for a few moments. Remove from fire and keep aside. Mix the salt and rice flour in the buttermilk. Pour the buttermilk into the same vessel. Add the fried seasoning. Add the vegetables when the sambar begins to boil. Add cooked dhal. Let it mix well. Boil and remove from fire. Tap ginger lightly with a rolling pin and add. Garnish with coriander and curry leaves.

Ingredients

Vegetable ¼ kg
Salt 1 tsp
Red gram dhal ⅝ cup
Oil 3 tsp
Mustard seeds ½ tsp
Fenugreek seeds ½ tsp
Dry red chillies 8
Green chillies 6
Rice flour 1 tsp
Buttermilk (Sour) 1 cup
Ginger 1" piece
Coriander leaves
(Finely chopped) 3-4 tbsp
Curry leaves 5-6

To serve 4 persons

VEGETABLE STEW
(VATRAL KUZHAMBU)

Ingredients

Vegetable 1/4 kg
Old tamarind A big lump the size of a lime
Mustard seeds 1/2 tsp
Fenugreek seeds 1/2 tsp
Dry red chillies 23
Red gram dhal 1/2 tsp
Asafoetida powder A pinch or to taste
Salt 1 1/2 tsp
Curry leaves 8-10
Sambar powder 2 1/2 tsp
Rice flour 1 tsp
Water 2 1/2 cups
Oil 4-5 tsp

To serve 4 persons

Vegetables like brinjal, lady's finger, onion, sweet potatoes, pumpkin, radish, cluster beans and runner beans can be used. Wash and chop the vegetable. Keep aside. If onions are being used, they can be sautéed in a little oil before adding.

Soak the tamarind in the water for about 20 minutes and prepare tamarind juice.

Heat the oil in a heavy, e.g. stoneware, vessel. Fry mustard, fenugreek, broken and pinched red chillies, red gram dhal and asafoetida. Add the tamarind juice. Add curry leaves and the cut vegetable along with the sambar powder. Fry to a reddish colour. Add salt. Boil till the soup reduces to 2 cups. Mix the rice flour with water. Add to the 'kuzhambu'. Boil and remove from fire.

Note:

Fried pappads ('appalams') broken into bits can be added before serving. 'Kuzhambu curry vadam' (wafers) may also be fried and added to enrich the flavour.

BUTTERMILK STEW
(MOAR KUZHAMBU)

Vegetables like Bangalore brinjal, brinjal, ash gourd, drumstick or lady's finger can be used in preparing this recipe. Wash and cut the vegetable being used. If using ash gourd, drumstick or Bangalore brinjal, cook in water with salt before adding. If using lady's finger or brinjal, fry lightly in oil with salt before adding. Potatoes and colocasia may also be used. Boil in their jackets, peel, cut into large bits and add. Keep aside.

Soak the dhals and rice together in 1/4 cup water for a few minutes. Grind into a smooth paste with green chillies, cumin seeds, coconut and curry leaves

Add the ground paste and salt to the buttermilk and mix well. Put the mixture in a vessel and boil over a slow fire, stirring all the time with a ladle. When boiled, add the cooked vegetables. When the stew is still on the fire, add a few curry leaves. Remove from fire. Heat the oil in a frying pan. Fry red chillies and mustard, and the coriander seeds, if used. Add to the stew as seasoning. Garnish with coriander leaves.

Note:
Approximately 3/4-1 cup of grated coconut, cumin seeds and green chillies may be ground without the dhals or only Bengal gram dhal may be used, excluding red gram dhal. Rice may be replaced by 1/2 tsp rice flour.

Ingredients

Vegetable 1/4 kg
Salt 1 1/2 tsp
Red gram dhal 1/2 tsp
Bengal gram dhal 1 tsp
Rice 1/2 tsp
Green chillies 4-5
Cumin seeds 1/4 tsp
Coconut (Grated) 1/4 cup
Curry leaves (Broken) 3 tbsp
Buttermilk (Slightly sour) 2 cups
Gingelly oil 2 tsp
Dry red chillies 2
Mustard seeds 1 tsp
Coriander seeds 1/2 tsp (Optional)
Coriander leaves (Finely chopped) 3 tbsp

To serve 4 persons

Salted and dried berries ('manaithakkali', 'chundaikai' or 'thummattikai') may be fried and added to the stew.

Sambar wafers or vadams may also be fried and added.

Alternatively, soak 1/2 cup of combined Bengal gram dhal, red gram dhal and black gram dhal. Wash and drain. Grind with salt and red chillies. Prepare small round balls (like 'bondas') with this paste. Fry and add to the stew.

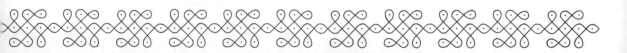

DHAL STEW
(PORITHA KUZHAMBU)

A variety of vegetables can be used such as snake gourd, Bangalore brinjal, drumstick, ridge gourd and runner beans. Alternatively, brinjal, cluster beans and amaranth stems may also be used.

Cook the dhal. (See Sambar recipe on p. 3.) Keep aside. Cut the vegetable. Wash and cook in water, with salt. Add sambar powder. When the vegetables are well cooked, add the cooked dhal. Let the mixture boil well. Add ground coconut. Mix the rice flour in water and add. Boil for a few minutes. Add the asafoetida. Boil for one second. Garnish with curry leaves. Remove from fire. Heat oil in a frying pan and fry mustard and black gram dhal. Use to season the 'kuzhambu'.

Note:
Both dhals together may also be used.

To serve convalescing patients, do not add coconut. Season with 1/4 tsp cumin seeds in addition to mustard and black gram dhal.

If cluster beans is used, it should be fried a little before boiling. When sabre beans and amaranth stems are used, a handful of beans seed pulse may be cooked separately and added.

Ingredients

Red gram dhal or green gram dhal 1/2 cup
Vegetable 150 gms
Water 1 1/2 cups
Salt 3/4 tsp
Sambar powder 1/2 tsp
Coconut (Ground) 4 tbsp
Rice flour 1/2 tsp
Asafoetida powder A pinch or to taste
Curry leaves (Broken) 2 tbsp
Oil 2 tsp
Mustard seeds 1/2 tsp
Black gram dhal 1/2 tsp

To serve 4 persons

MIXED VEGETABLE STEW
(EZHUKARI KUZHAMBU)

Ingredients

Vegetables (Combined)
4 cups
Red gram dhal ¾ cup
Tamarind A big lump the size
of an orange
Oil 12 tsp
Bengal gram dhal ⅛ cup
Dry red chillies 18-22
Coconut ½ (Large)
Coriander seeds ¼ cup
Mustard seeds 2 tsp
Fenugreek seeds 1½ tsp
Asafoetida powder A pinch
or to taste
Curry leaves 15-20
Salt 2 tbsp
Turmeric powder ½ tsp
Rice flour 2 tsp
Coriander leaves (Chopped)
¼ cup

To serve 4 persons

For the vegetables, you can choose from fresh bean seeds (raw), ash gourd, pumpkin, sweet potatoes, plantains, brinjal, snake gourd, sabre beans, cluster beans, French beans, Bangalore brinjal, yam, colocasia, potatoes and green chillies. Sometimes drumstick and ribbed gourd are also included. A few lady's fingers may also be used.

Cook the red gram dhal dhal till very soft.
(See Sambar recipe on p. 3.)

Prepare tamarind juice. Soak the tamarind in 2 cups water for 20 to 30 minutes. Squeeze it out, adding water little by little to prepare 2-3 cups of juice.

Heat 5-6 tsp of oil in a frying pan. Fry the Bengal gram dhal, 15-18 red chillies, coconut and coriander seeds to a reddish colour and grind into a smooth paste. Keep aside.

In the same frying pan, heat another 5-6 tsp of oil. Fry mustard, fenugreek seeds, remaining red chillies, asafoetida powder and curry leaves. Keep aside.

Scrape skin from yam and cut into small bits. Boil with potatoes and colacasia in their jackets. Peel skin from potatoes and colacasia. Cut into two or three bits. Cut all other vegetables except cluster beans more or less to the same size. Pinch each cluster bean into two and fry a little. Add a little water and cook with bean seeds. When half-cooked, add the other vegetables with salt

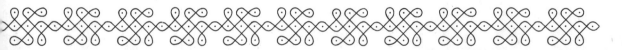

and turmeric power. When the vegetables begin to cook properly, turn with a spoon. When half-boiled, pour in tamarind juice. Boil well till the vegetables are soft. Add cooked red gram dhal and the ground paste. Mix thoroughly. Add fried seasonings. Mix the rice flour in water. Add and mix well with the boiling 'kuzhambu'. Let it boil till all the ingredients mix well. Add coriander leaves. Serve hot.

Note:

This 'kuzhambu' will be rather thick. More dhal can be added to make the preparation a little thinner to be served like a sambar.

RASAM
(PARUPPU RASAM)

Ingredients

Tamarind *A lump the size of a small lime*

Tomato *1 (Medium) (Optional)*

Red gram dhal *1/4 cup (May be increased to 1/3 cup)*

Salt *1 1/2 tsp*

Sambar powder *1 tsp*

Asafoetida *A pinch or to taste*

Curry leaves *8-10*

Oil or ghee *2 tsp*

Mustard seeds *1 tsp*

Dry red chillies *2*

Coriander leaves *(Chopped) 1/4 cup*

To serve *4 persons*

Photograph on p. 10

Soak the tamarind in 1 cup water for 20 minutes. Squeeze it out, adding water a little at a time to prepare 2 cups of juice.

Cook the red gram dhal till very soft. (See Sambar recipe on p. 3.) Prepare 1/2 a cup of 'dhal water'. (Add enough water when cooking the dhal. Decant the water to get 'dhal water'.) Mash the softly cooked dhal and mix well with the remaining water. Keep aside.

Pour the tamarind juice into a vessel. Add salt, sambar powder, asafoetida and curry leaves. Add the 'dhal water'. Cover the vessel and place on the fire. Boil well till the smell of sambar powder goes. If using tomato, cut into four pieces and add to the boiling tamarind water before adding dhal. Add mashed dhal. Boil for a minute or two. Add enough plain water or 'dhal water' to make 4 cups of rasam. Wait till the rasam bubbles and froths up. Remove from fire. Heat oil/ghee in a frying pan. Fry mustard and red chillies. Season the rasam. Garnish with curry leaves and coriander leaves.

Note:
When tomato is used, decrease the quantity of tamarind accordingly.

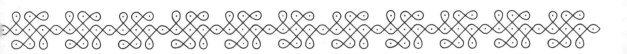

MYSORE RASAM

Prepare 2 cups of tamarind juice. (See Rasam recipe on p. 14.) Cook the red gram dhal dhal till very soft. (See Sambar recipe on p. 3.) Prepare 4 cups of 'dhal water'. (Add enough water when cooking the dhal. Decant the water to prepare 'dhal water'.) Keep the cooked dhal and 'dhal water' aside separately.

Heat 2 tsp of oil in a frying pan. Fry the coriander seeds, Bengal gram dhal and 8 red chillies till they turn light brown. Powder these with the peppercorns.

Pour the tamarind juice in a vessel. Add salt and asafoetida. Add a few pinched curry leaves. Cover the vessel and place on fire. Bring to boil. If using tomato, cut into four pieces and add to the boiling tamarind water before adding the dhal. Add the cooked dhal and boil well. Add the 'dhal-water'. Wait till rasam froths up. Remove from fire. Add the prepared powder. Mix well with a spoon. Heat the ghee and 1 tsp of oil in a frying pan. Fry mustard and remaining red chillies. Pinch the curry leaves and fry for a few seconds. When the mustard splutters, remove from fire and season the rasam. Garnish with coriander leaves.

Note:
When tomato is used, decrease the quantity of tamarind accordingly.

Ingredients

Tamarind *A lump the size of a lime*
Red gram dhal *½ cup*
Oil *3 tsp*
Coriander seeds *1½ tbsp*
Bengal gram dhal *2 tsp*
Dry red chillies *10*
Black peppercorns *5-6*
Salt *1½ tsp*
Asafoetida powder *A pinch or to taste*
Curry leaves *2 tbsp*
Tomato *1 (Medium) (Optional)*
Ghee *1 tsp*
Mustard seeds *1 tsp*
Coriander leaves *4 tbsp*

To serve *4 persons*

PEPPER & CUMIN RASAM
(JEERA MOLAGU RASAM)

Ingredients

Tamarind *A lump the size of a lime*

Salt *1½ tsp*

Rasam powder *½ tsp*

Water *1 cup*

Red gram dhal *1 tsp*

Cumin seeds *¾ tsp*

Black peppercorns *(Crushed) ½ tsp*

Curry leaves *8-10*

Ghee *2 tsp*

Mustard seeds *1 tsp*

Dry red chillies *2*

To serve *4 persons*

Add the tamarind, salt and rasam powder to the water. Coarsely grind the dhal in a mixie/food processor. Add along with the cumin seeds and crushed pepper. Add a few pinched curry leaves. Cover the vessel and place on fire. Boil well till the smell of rasam powder goes. Add a further 1/2 cup to 1 cup water. Wait till the rasam froths up. Remove froth.

Heat ghee in a pan. Fry mustard, red chillies and curry leaves. Season the rasam.

Note:

This rasam can be prepared without using rasam powder at all. If rasam powder is not being used, take an additional 1 tsp pepper. Crush it. Add to the rasam. Season with 4 extra dry red chillies.

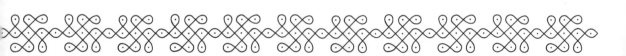

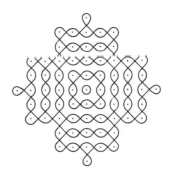

VEGETABLES

PITLAY

Fry coriander seeds, 1 tsp Bengal gram dhal, 3/4 tsp black gram dhal, 6 red chillies and grated coconut till golden brown in 1 tsp oil. Grind to a paste (which should not be very smooth). Keep aside.

Prepare 2 1/2-3 cups tamarind juice. (See Rasam recipe on p.14.) Cook the red gram dhal till very soft. (See Sambar recipe on p.3.)

A variety of vegetables like Bangalore brinjal, brinjals, drumstick, cluster beans, sabre beans, yam or potatoes may be used in making 'pitlay'. If brinjals, Bangalore brinjal or drumsticks are used, wash and cut the vegetable into small pieces and boil in the prepared tamarind water, with salt. If cluster beans are used, cut and fry lightly before boiling in water. When cooked, add the tamarind juice. In the case of sabre beans, cut the vegetable and add to boiling water with salt. When cooked, add tamarind juice. If using yam or potato, cut and boil separately and then add to tamarind juice.

To the cooked vegetable in the vessel, add the cooked red gram dhal and the prepared paste. Bring to boil. Thicken with rice flour, mixed in water, if necessary. Boil for a few seconds. Heat the remaining oil in a frying pan. Fry mustard, 3/4 tsp black gram dhal and 2 dry red chillies. Add the fried seasonings to the 'pitlay'. Garnish with curry and coriander leaves.
Add asafoetida water. Serve hot.

Ingredients

Coriander seeds *1 1/2 tsp*
Bengal gram dhal *1 tsp*
Black gram dhal *1 1/2 tsp*
Dry red chillies *8*
Coconut *(Grated) 6 tbsp*
Oil *1 tbsp*
New tamarind *A lump the size of a small lemon*
Red gram dhal *1/2 cup*
Vegetable *150-200 gms*
Salt *3-4 tsp*
Rice flour *1/4 tsp (Optional)*
Mustard seeds *1/2 tsp*
Curry leaves *(Broken) 2 tbsp*
Coriander leaves *(Chopped) 2-3 tbsp*
Asafoetida water *1 tsp*

To serve *4 persons*

CABBAGE BAAJI

Ingredients

Red gram dhal ¼ cup

Cabbage 175 gms

Salt 2 tsp

Green chillies 6

Rice flour ¼ tsp (Optional)

Oil 2 tsp

Mustard seeds ½ tsp

Ginger 1"-2" piece

Cashewnuts 6

Coriander leaves (Chopped)
1 tbsp

Curry leavves 5-6

Lime 1

Asafoetida water ½-1 tsp

To serve 4 persons

Photograph on p. 27

Cook the dhal till very soft. (See Sambar recipe on p.3.)

Shred cabbage. Cook in water with salt till tender. Fry the green chillies lightly and add to the cabbage. Add cooked dhal. If the preparation is a little watery, thicken with rice flour mixed in water. Boil for a few minutes. Remove from fire. Heat oil in a frying pan. Fry mustard, chopped ginger and cashewnuts. Season the cabbage. Garnish with curry and coriander leaves. Add lime juice and asafoetida water to enhance flavour. Serve hot.

CARROT BAAJI

Scrape the skin off the carrot. Cut into fine pieces. Cook the carrot in water with salt and turmeric powder. When well cooked, drain water. Heat 1/2 tsp oil in a frying pan and fry the anise seed. Powder the fried anise seed and keep aside. Heat the remaining oil in a frying pan. Fry the mustard and black gram dhal. To this add the cooked carrot, chilli powder and anise powder. Fry well and serve.

Alternatively, cook the red gram dhal till very soft. Cook the cut carrot along with salt and turmeric powder. Add the cooked dhal and grated coconut to the cooked carrots. Heat 4 tsp oil in a frying pan. Fry mustard and black gram dhal and season.

Ingredients

Carrot *350 gms*
Salt *1¼ tsp*
Turmeric powder *¼ tsp*
Oil *4 tsp*
Anise seeds *1 tsp*
Mustard seeds *1 tsp*
Black gram dhal *2 tsp*
Chilli powder *1 tsp*
Red gram dhal *½ cup*
(Optional)
Coconut *(Grated) ¼ cup*
(Optional)

To serve *4 persons*

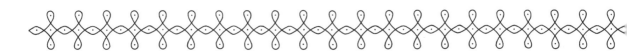

YAM MASIYAL

(SENAI MASIYAL)

Ingredients

Red gram dhal ¼ cup

Tamarind A lump the size of
an arecanut

Yam 175 gms

Baking soda A pinch
(Optional)

Salt 1¼ tsp

Turmeric powder ¼ tsp

Oil 4 tsp

Mustard seeds ¼ tsp

Black gram dhal 1 tsp

Green chillies 5-6

Ginger 1"-2" piece

Asafoetida A pinch or to taste

Coconut milk ⅕ cup

Curry leaves 8-10

Coriander leaves 2 tbsp

To serve 4 persons

Cook the red gram dhal till vey soft. (See Sambar recipe
on p.3.) Prepare tamarind juice. (See Rasam recipe
on p.14.)

Scrape skin from yam and cut into small pieces. Wash
thoroughly. Put in ¹/2 cup to 1 cup boiling water and
cook well, then drain. Baking soda may be added, if
necessary, to soften the yam. Mash yam by hand. Mix
tamarind juice, salt and turmeric powder with yam.
Heat oil in a frying pan. Fry mustard and black gram
dhal. Add green chillies and chopped ginger and fry.
Add mashed yam and tamarind mixture. Add cooked
red gram dhal. Add asafoetida and boil. Add coconut
milk and pinched curry leaves. Bring to boil twice more.
Remove from fire. Garnish with coriander leaves
and serve hot.

STEAMED DHAL CURRY
(PARUPPU PUTTU)

Soak the red gram dhal. Wash and drain off water. Grind with the red chillies, asafoetida and salt. Do not add too much water. The paste should be smooth and firm.

Heat water in an idli vessel or a pan. Use a single idli tray. Smear a plantain leaf with oil. Keep it on the tray. Spread the dough on that. Cover with a lid. Steam for about 20 minutes. Open the lid and insert a fork into the dough. If the dough does not stick to it, it is cooked. (If it sticks, keep it covered and cook for some more time.) Remove the cooked mass. Cool and crumble into a powder.

Heat the oil in a frying pan. Add mustard and let it splutter. Add the crumbled dhal with curry leaves. Turn four or five times. Remove from fire and serve.

Note:
Plantain flower, cabbage, cluster beans, French beans, etc., can be cut and cooked separately and added to the crumbled dhal along with the seasoning.

Ingredients

Red gram dhal 2 cups
Dry red chillies 10-12
Asafoetida powder A pinch
or to taste
Salt 2 tsp
Oil 7-8 tsp
Mustard seeds 2 tsp
Curry leaves 8-10

To serve 4 persons

BRINJAL FRY
(KATHIRIKAI VADHAKAL)

Ingredients

Tender brinjal 700 gms
Salt 2 tsp
Chilli powder 2½ tsp
Ghee 2 tsp
Bengal gram flour ½ cup
Asafoetida water ½-1 tsp
Tamarind A lump the size of
an arecanut
Gingelly oil 1½ cups

To serve 4 persons

Split open the brinjals into two and cut into bits of medium thickness. Wash and drain out the water. Mix the salt, chilli powder and ghee with Bengal gram flour. Mix asafoetida water with the washed and cut vegetable. Prepare a thick tamarind juice. Sprinkle this juice over the cut brinjals and mix well. Divide the brinjals and Bengal gram flour into four portions. Now, mix each portion of the brinjals with each part of the Bengal gram flour mixture. Keep aside.

Heat oil in a frying pan. Put in a small lump of tamarind and when the oil is heated properly, remove the tamarind lump. Take one part of the mixed brinjal and flour and fry it in the oil, turning often. Remove when crisp. Repeat with the second part. Put a small tamarind lump in the remaining oil, remove as before when oil is heated and fry the brinjal bits till crisp. Repeat for the rest of the portions.

Note:

Due to the Bengal gram flour, the oil will turn thick while deep frying. So it is advisable not to heat all the oil at one go but to heat as much oil as required to fry each portion of the vegetable.

If very tender brinjals are available, there may be no need to mix them with tamarind juice, although when mixed with tamarind juice, the brinjals do taste better.

MASALA BRINJAL
(ENNAI KATHIRIKAI)

Heat 2 tsp oil in a frying pan. Fry the red chillies, coriander seeds and the dhals to a reddish brown. Keep aside. Grate the coconut and fry in 2 tsp oil to a reddish brown. Powder the fried chillies and coriander seeds with the salt. Add the fried dhals and fried coconut. Powder once again. Add asafoetida powder. Mix well and keep the powder separate.

Select very tender, fresh and small brinjals of uniform size. Wash the brinjals. Cut out the stem and slit the brinjal in four from the top. Take care that the brinjal does not get cut into four pieces, but is only slit. Check to see that there are no insects or worms inside the brinjals. Stuff each brinjal with the prepared powder, a little at a time.

Heat 5-6 tsp of oil. Add mustard. When it splutters, add stuffed brinjals. Sprinkle a little water, if necessary. (If brinjals are very tender, there is no need for water.) Cover with a plate. Cook till very soft, turning the brinjals quite often.

Note:
If the brinjals are not very tender and have seeds, soak a marble-size piece of tamarind in 1/2 cup of water, prepare the juice and sprinkle this tamarind juice instead of plain water.

Ingredients

Oil 10 tsp
Dry red chillies 6
Brinjal 350 gms
Coriander seeds 3 tsp
Bengal gram dhal 1½ tsp
Black gram dhal 1½ tsp
Coconut ¼ (Medium)
Salt 1½ tsp
Asafoetida powder A pinch
or to taste
Mustard seeds 1-2 tsp

To serve 4 persons

COLOCASIA FRY

(SEPPANGKIZHANGU VADHAKAL)

Ingredients

Colocasia *350 gms*

Oil *4 tsp*

Mustard seeds *1 tsp*

Black gram dhal *2 tsp*

Green chillies *4-6*

Tamarind *A lump the size of an arecanut*

Turmeric powder *½ tsp*

Salt *1½ tsp*

Asafoetida water *1 tsp*

Curry leaves *8-10*

Rice flour *2 tsp*

To serve *4 persons*

Wash the colocasia well. Boil in their jackets. Peel. Cut into fairly big pieces, i.e., cut each colocasia into two or three bits.

Heat oil in a frying pan. Fry the mustard and black gram dhal. Add chopped green chillies. Fry a little, and then add the colocasia pieces. Prepare ½ to ¾ cup tamarind juice and add to the colocasia. Add salt and turmeric powder along with asafoetida water and pinched curry leaves. Turn three or four times. Boil for a while. Add rice flour mixed in water and fry together. Keep on the fire for a while. When it becomes a mass, remove from fire.

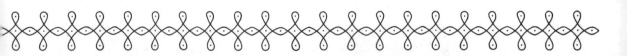

COLOCASIA LEAF CURRY

(SEPPANGKIZHANGU ELAI PORIYAL)

Soak the first four dhals, which altogether measure 1 cup, for over an hour, wash well and drain water. Grind the dhals with the salt, red chillies and asafoetida into a smooth and firm paste (sprinkling just enough water).

The colocasia leaves should be of a very good variety and tender (and not very mature). Cut and discard the stalk. Wash and wipe the leaves. Invert each leaf on the counter. Spread the paste (a handful) evenly on the back of each leaf. Roll tightly. Increase or decrease the quantity of paste according to the size of the leaves and the rolls.

Heat water in a pan or idli vessel. Insert a single idli tray covered with a thin white cloth. Arrange the rolled leaves on it. (Place only as many leaves as the tray can hold.) Close the vessel and steam the leaves. When the leaves are cooked, beads of water will drip from the lid. Open the lid and see whether the leaves have changed colour. Test and see if the paste has also cooked. Remove the steamed leaves on a tray. Steam the rest of the leaves, taking care that there is enough water for steaming.

After cooling, cut each roll into ten or twelve bits. Heat the oil in a frying pan. Season with mustard and black gram dhal. Add the cut steamed colocasia leaves and fry, turning often. Remove from fire and serve.

Ingredients

Red gram dhal ¼ cup
Bengal gram dhal ¼ cup
Black gram dhal ¼ cup
Green gram dhal ¼ cup
Salt 2 tsp
Dry red chillies 8
Asafoetida A pinch or to taste
Colocasia leaves 8 (Medium sized)
Oil ⅕ to ¼ cup
Mustard seeds 1 tsp
Black gram dhal 2 tsp

To serve 4 persons

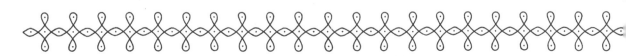

MASHED POTATO
(ORULAIKIZHANGU PODI)

Ingredients

Oil 4 tsp
Dry red chillies 6-8
Red gram dhal 2 tsp
Black gram dhal 2 tsp
Asafoetida A pinch or to taste
Mustard seeds ½ tsp
Salt 1½ tsp
Potato 350 gms (Large)

Heat the oil in a frying pan. Fry the red chillies, red gram dhal, black gram dhal, asafoetida and mustard till they turn reddish brown in colour. Remove from fire. When cool, powder coarsely with salt in a mixie/ food processor

Boil the potatoes in their jackets. Peel. Mash the boiled potatoes. Add the coarse powder to the mashed pototoes. Mix well and serve hot.

To serve 4 persons

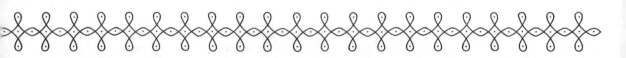

MASALA POTATO

Heat 2 tsp of oil in a frying pan. Fry the poppy seeds, cinnamon, anise seeds, cloves and cardamoms. Powder and keep masala aside. Boil the potatoes in their jackets. Peel and cut. Peel onions and chop. Heat the remaining oil in a frying pan. Fry the mustard and black gram dhal. Add chopped ginger, green chillies and onions and fry. Add potato bits, turmeric powder and salt. Mix and turn three or four times. Soak the Bengal gram flour in the water. Pour into the pan and mix well. Sprinkle powdered masala over the 'curry' and add the ghee. Mix and turn. Cook till it becomes a thick mass. Remove. Serve as a side dish with 'poori'. (See recipe on p. 70.)

Note:

The powdered masala can be replaced with asafoetida powder and curry leaves.

The dish may be prepared without onions as well.

Ingredients

Oil 7-8 tsp

Poppy seeds 1/2 tsp

Cinnamon 1/2" piece

Anise seeds 1/2 tsp

Cloves 4

Green cardamoms 4

Potato 350 gms

Onion 100 gms

Mustard seeds 1 tsp

Black gram dhal 1 1/2 tsp

Ginger A marble-sized bit

Green chillies 6-8

Turmeric powder 1/4 tsp

Salt 1 1/2 tsp

Bengal gram flour 1/2 cup

Water 1/2 cup

Ghee 2 tsp

To serve 4 persons

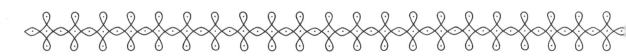

PUMPKIN CURRY

(POOSHNIKAI PORIYAL)

Ingredients

Pumpkin (Ripe) 150 gms

Salt ¼ tsp

Turmeric powder ¼-½ tsp

Coconut ¼ (Medium)

Oil 4 tsp

Mustard seeds ½ tsp

Black gram dhal 1 tsp

Dry red chillies 2-3

Jaggery A lump the size of a lime

Rice flour 2 tsp

To serve 4 persons

Remove skin from the pumpkin and cut into small arecanut-sized pieces. Wash the cut pumpkin. Add 1 to 1½ cups water . Add salt and turmeric powder and boil. Turn twice or thrice, when the vegetable boils vigorously. Remove from fire when properly cooked. The vegetable should be soft.

Grate coconut and keep aside. Heat oil in a frying pan. Fry mustard, black gram dhal and red chillies. Add the boiled vegetable and jaggery. When the jaggery begins to melt, add grated coconut and rice flour mixed in water. Cook for a few minutes, turning the vegetable four to five times. Remove from fire and serve.

SWEET POTATO CURRY

(SAKKARAIVALLIKIZHANGHU VADHAKAL)

Cut the vegetable into slices. (Do not peel.) Wash well to
remove any mud and sand. Boil just enough water to
cover the vegetable in a heavy vessel. Add the sliced and
washed vegetable. Add salt. Cook for a while. Turn and
cook a little more. Remove from fire. Strain out the water.

Heat oil in a frying pan and fry mustard, black gram
dhal and red chillies. Add the cooked vegetable with the
jaggery or sugar. Fry for a few minutes and remove
from fire.

Ingredients

Sweet potato 350 gms
Salt ½ tsp
Oil 2-3 tsp
Mustard seeds ½ tsp
Black gram dhal 1 tsp
Dry red chillies 2
Jaggery A marble-sized lump
or Sugar 1 tsp

To serve 4 persons

BITTER GOURD CURRY

(PAVAKKAI PORIYAL)

Ingredients

Bitter gourd *200 gms*

Tamarind *A lump the size*
of a marble

Salt *1½ tsp*

Turmeric powder *½ tsp*

Jaggery *A marble-sized lump*

Oil *5-6 tsp*

Mustard seeds *1 tsp*

Chilli powder *1½ tsp*

Asafoetida water *½ tsp*

To serve *4 persons*

Cut the bitter gourd into half-inch long pieces. If they are of the small variety, cut out the stem and just slit the gourd or cut into two halves lengthwise. Boil 1 to 2 cups water. Add the bitter gourd. Do not cook the bitter gourd too well. Strain out the water. Prepare 1/2 to 3/4 cup thick tamarind juice. Add the tamarind juice to the half-cooked vegetable with the salt and turmeric powder. When the vegetable turns soft, add the jaggery. Cook till all the water is absorbed. Remove from fire and keep aside.

Heat oil in a frying pan. Season with mustard. Add the cooked bitter gourd along with the chilli powder and asafoetida water. Fry over a slow fire. Turn now and then. Fry well and remove from fire.

Note:

As an alternative, 2 tsp sambar powder can be added to the tamarind juice when cooking the bitter gourd. In this case, omit the red chilli powder and use mustard and black gram dhal for seasoning.

The bitter gourd can also be cooked straightaway in the thick tamarind juice along with salt, turmeric powder and jaggery all together and then fried with the seasonings.

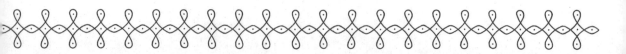

AVIYAL

Almost any vegetable can be used for this—snake gourd, sabre beans, cluster beans, drumstick, French beans, Bangalore brinjal, brinjal, plantain, amaranth stem, carrot, ash gourd, cucumber, potatoes and yam—except colocasia and lady's finger. If colocasia is used, boil a few, peel and add separately. It is not necessary that all vegetables should be used. Use them in similar quantities to make up at least 4 cups when cut.

Wash and cut vegetables. Put water in a vessel and bring to boil. When water begins to boil, first put in those vegetables which normally take a longer time to cook (such as ash gourd, Bangalore brinjal, etc). After a few minutes, add the other vegetables including the mango, if being used. Finally, add salt and cover. When the vegetables begin to cook, turn once or twice. Cook all vegetables evenly. When well cooked, pour out excess water, if any. It is preferable to cut and boil potatoes separately. Cook potatoes in their jackets, peel and then add to the other vegetables. Potatoes can however also be boiled along with the other vegetables. But yam should always be cooked separately and added afterwards. Scrape yam. Cut into long bits (the same size as other vegetables) and cook. Cluster beans may be fried slightly before boiling.

Grate coconut and grind into a paste with cumin seeds, green chillies and rice. Mix with the curd. If mango is

Ingredients

Vegetables (Cut) *4 cups*
Green Mango *1* (Optional)
Salt *2 tsp*
Coconut ½ (Large)
Cumin seeds ½ tsp
Green chillies 4 5
Rice ½ tsp
Curd (Slightly sour) *1 cup*
Curry leaves *8-10*
Coconut oil ⅛ cup

To serve *4 persons*

Photograph on p. 28

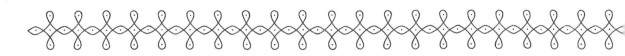

being used as a vegetable, reduce quantity of curd accordingly (as the mango itself will be sour). Add the curd mixture to the cooked vegetable. Mix well and boil. Remove from fire. Garnish with curry leaves. Pour raw coconut oil from the top. Mix well and serve.

Note:

If raw coconut oil is not preferred, heat the oil in a frying pan. Fry curry leaves in it and then pour into the 'aviyal'.

If the required quantities of mango and curd are not available, add 5-6 tbsp tamarind water when boiling the vegetables.

'Aviyal' can also be prepared with plantains, plantain stem, amaranth stem, Bangalore brinjal and ash gourd, each used separately.

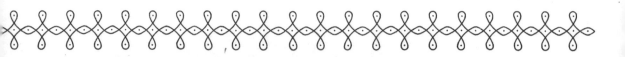

COCONUT KOOTTU

(THENGAI KOOTTU)

Plantain, amaranth stem, pumpkin and ash gourd can be used to prepare this dish. Cut the chosen vegetable into small squares of 1/2" length. Cook in water with salt. When cooked, drain off excess water.

Grind grated coconut, cumin seeds, green chillies and rice into a smooth paste . Add the ground paste to the cooked vegetables. Mix well and boil. Add raw coconut oil or gingelly oil from the top, reserving 1 tsp.

Heat 1 tsp oil in a frying pan. Fry mustard and black gram dhal and season the 'koottu'.

Note:

A little rice flour mixed in water may be added to the ground paste instead of grinding the rice.

Ingredients

Vegetable 100-150 gms
Salt 2 tbsp
Coconut (Grated) 1/4-1/2 cup
Cumin seeds 1 tbsp
Green chillies 2
Rice 1 tsp
Coconut oil or gingelly oil 1/2-1 tbsp
Mustard seeds 1 tsp
Black gram dhal 1/2 tsp

To serve 4 persons

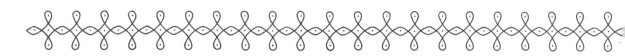

CLUSTER BEANS JAGGERY KOOTTU
(KOTHAVARAKKAI VELLA KOOTTU)

Ingredients

Cluster beans *350 gms*

Coconut *½ (Medium)*

Tamarind *A lump the size of a small lime*

Oil *5-6 tsp*

Salt *1½ tsp*

Turmeric powder *½-¾ tsp*

Sambar powder *2 tsp*

Jaggery *A lump the size of a big lime*

Asafoetida water *½ -1 tsp*

Curry leaves *8-10*

Rice flour *2-3 tsp*

Bengal gram dhal *2 tsp*

Black gram dhal *2 tsp*

Mustard *1 tsp*

To serve *4 persons*

Wash the cluster beans and cut into very small pieces. Either grate or finely chop the coconut. Prepare 1/4 cup thick tamarind juice. Heat 3-4 tsp oil in a frying pan. Add the beans along with the salt and turmeric powder. Fry for a while. Cover the vegetable with water. Add sambar powder. Cook till tender. Add thick tamarind juice and jaggery. Allow jaggery to melt and mix well. Add the asafoetida water and curry leaves. Mix rice flour with water and add.

Heat remaining oil in a separate frying pan. Fry mustard, black gram dhal, bengal gram dhal and grated/chopped coconut to a reddish brown colour. Add to the vegetable. Remove from fire and serve.

Note:
Bean seeds, fresh or dry, may be cooked and added to the dish.

This dish can also be made with French beans, sabre beans, brinjal, plantain flower and Bangalore brinjal.

TENDER PUMPKIN MILK KOOTTU
(CHIINA ELAM PARANGHIKAI KOOTTU)

Choose small tender pumpkin only. Remove skin. Wash
the vegetable. Cut into thin long fingers (about
1/4 inch). Heat 1/4 to 1/2 cup water in a vessel. Cook the
pumpkin with salt in the water. (Do not allow it to get
too tender.) Add the sugar. Let it mix well. Mix rice flour
in the milk and add. Boil for a few seconds and remove.

Heat oil in a frying pan. Fry mustard, black gram dhal
and chillies and season the cooked vegetables.

Note:
Coconut milk can be used instead of milk or equal
quantities of milk and coconut milk may be used.

When the vegetable has cooked, drain excess water
before adding sugar and milk.

Ingredients

Pumpkin 200 gms
Salt A pinch
Sugar 2 tbsp
Rice flour 2 tsp
Milk 1/2 cup
Oil 2 tsp
Mustard seeds 1/2 tsp
Black gram dhal 1 tsp
Dry red chillies 2
or green chillies 2

To serve 4 persons

RICE

COCONUT RICE

(THENGAI SAADHAM)

Cook the rice and spread on a plate to cool.

Soak black gram dhal in 1/4 cup water and wash. Drain out the water completely. Grate the coconut. Break cashewnuts into small bits. Chop green chillies. Soak asafoetida in water to prepare asafoetida water.

Heat oil in a frying pan. Add mustard, red chillies and asafoetida water. Add the cashewnuts when the mustard begins to splutter, and fry. Add the soaked dhal. Fry well till the water is absorbed. Add the grated coconut and fry till the coconut turns reddish brown. Add the curry leaves. Stir for a minute or two. Remove from fire.

Mix with cooled rice and salt. Pour ghee over the rice before serving.

Ingredients

Rice 1½ cups
Black gram dhal 1 tbsp
Coconut ½ (Large)
Cashewnuts 12
Green chillies 3
Asafoetida A pinch or to taste
Oil 6 tsp
Mustard seeds 1 tsp
Dry red chillies 3
Curry leaves (Broken) 2 tbsp
Salt 1½ tsp
Ghee 2-3 tsp

To serve 4 persons

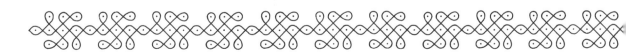

Lemon Rice

(ELIMICHAM PAZHAM SAADHAM)

Ingredients

Rice 1½ cups

Oil 7-8 tsp

Bengal gram dhal 1 tbsp

Lime 2 (Medium)

Turmeric powder ¼ tsp

Salt ¼ tsp

Green chillies 4-5

Mustard seeds 1 tsp

Dry red chillies 3

Asafoetida powder A pinch
or to taste

To serve 4 persons

Photograph on p. 45

Cook the rice and spread on a plate to cool. Mix 2-3 tsp of raw oil into the rice and break the lumps.

Soak Bengal gram dhal in a little water till it becomes soft. Drain water and keep soaked dhal aside. Squeeze the lime. Filter and keep juice aside. Add turmeric powder and salt to the lime juice. Chop green chillies. Heat the oil in a frying pan. Add mustard, red chillies and asafoetida. Add green chillies and fry. Add soaked dhal and fry till dry. Mix the seasoning with the lime juice. Mix with the cooled rice.

Note:

A couple of appalams can be fried and broken into bits and mixed with the rice before serving.

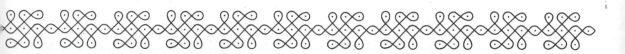

TAMARIND RICE

(PULIYODHARAI)

Cook the rice and spread on a plate to cool. Mix 2-3 tsp of raw oil into the rice and break the lumps.

Add 1/2 cup water, a little at a time to the tamarind and prepare a thick juice. Filter and keep the clean tamarind juice aside. Soak the dhal in a little water till it becomes soft. Wash and drain. Fry fenugreek seeds and asafoetida in a little oil and powder. Pinch the red chillies into small bits (of two or three).

Heat remaining oil in a heavy vessel. Fry mustard and pinched red chillies. Add soaked Bengal gram and fry till dry. Add turmeric powder. Pour in tamarind juice . Add salt and asafoetida and fenugreek powders and mix. Pinch the curry leaves and add. Boil well over a slow fire. Stir quite often to prevent scorching. When the sauce thickens and the water fully evaporates, oil will float on top. (The sauce will not be sticky.) When sufficiently boiled, remove from fire and cool. Pour enough of the sauce into the cooled rice and mix well.

Note:

Instead of Bengal gram, roasted groundnuts may be used. Winnow out the skin and add when the tamarind juice is boiling.

A stone vessel ('kalchatti') can be used to prepare the sauce, which will enhance the taste.

Ingredients

Rice *2 cups*

Oil *1/4 cup*

Tamarind *A lump the size of an orange or a big wood apple*

Bengal gram dhal *(Whole or pulse) 1/4 cup*

Fenugreek seeds *1 tsp*

Asafoetida powder *A pinch or to taste*

Dry red chillies *10-12*

Mustard seeds *2 tsp*

Turmeric powder *1/2 tsp*

Salt *1 1/2 tsp*

Curry leaves *(Broken) 2-3 tbsp*

To serve *4 persons*

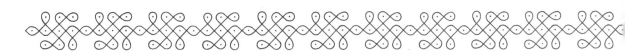

CURD RICE

(THAYIR SAADHAM)

Ingredients

Green chillies 2-3

Ginger 3" piece

Rice 2 cups

Curry leaves (Broken) 1 tbsp

Salt 2½-3 tsp

Curd 1 cup

Milk 1½ cups

Oil 2 tsp

Mustard seeds 1 tsp

Chop the green chillies and ginger. Keep aside. Cook the rice till very soft. Crumble the curry leaves with the salt and add to the rice. Mix well with the rice, using a spoon. The rice must be made pulpy. Add the curd and the milk. Should the rice be loose, increase the quantity of curd or milk or both. Mix well. Heat oil and fry the mustard. Add the chopped green chillies and ginger to the seasoned mustard and fry. Take off fire, add to the rice and mix.

To serve 4 persons

Photograph on p. 46

TIFFIN

RICE PONGAL

(VENN PONGAL)

Dry roast green gram dhal lightly. Wash and clean the dhal as also the rice. Boil the water in a vessel. Add the rice and dhal. Stir quite often as it cooks. When almost cooked, add salt and cook well. Remove from fire when the water is absorbed completely and the rice becomes very soft.

Prepare a coarse powder of the pepper and cumin seeds. Cut ginger into small pieces. Break the cashewnuts into small pieces. Heat the ghee in a frying pan. Fry the broken cashewnuts lightly. Add the pepper-cumin seeds powder. Fry for a few moments. Add ginger and fry for a while. Add the cooked 'pongal' and mix well. Serve hot.

Note:
Rice and dhal may be cooked together in a pressure cooker till very soft.

Ingredients

Green gram dhal 1/2 cup
Rice 1 cup
Water 3 cups
Black peppercorns 1 1/2 tsp
Cumin seeds 1 1/2 tsp
Salt 1 tsp
Ginger 1" piece
Cashewnuts 12
Ghee 1/4-1/2 cup

To serve 4 persons

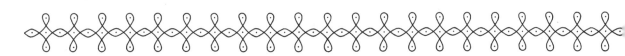

Sweet Pongal

(SAKKARE PONGAL)

Ingredients

Milk *1-3 cups*

Rice *2 cups*

Green gram dhal *3/4 cup*

Jaggery or sugar *3 cups*

Coconut *1/2 (Medium)*

Ghee *1/2 cup*

Cashewnuts *15-20*

Raisins *2-3 tbsp*

Nutmeg *1/2*

Saffron *1/4-1/2 tsp (to be used only with sugar)*

Green cardamoms *7-8*

Borneal flakes *1/4-1/2 tsp*

To serve *4 persons*

Mix the milk with water to make 7 1/2 cups (if new rice is being used) or 8 cups (if old rice is being used). Dry roast green gram dhal lightly. Take a heavy vessel. Smear the outside with a paste of rice flour. Boil water and milk mixture in it. Wash the rice and green gram dhal five or six times. Remove stones, if any, and drain completely. Add to the boiling milk and water mixture. Stir quite often. Cook till the rice becomes a very soft pulpy mass and the water is absorbed fully. (Do not strain out the water.) Add sugar or jaggery. Cook over a slow fire, turning it quite often to prevent sticking to the bottom. (You can add 4 tsp of ghee to prevent this.) Keep cooking till jaggery (or sugar) mixes well with the rice and the 'pongal' attains a sticky consistency.

Grate the coconut. Fry the cashewnuts, raisins and grated coconut in ghee till golden. Add to the 'pongal'. Grate the nutmeg and fry in ghee separately. Finely powder it after frying and add to the 'pongal'. Dissolve saffron in 1 tsp water or milk and add. Powder the cardamom. Add along with borneal flakes. Add 4 tsp of melted ghee. Remove from fire and serve.

Note:

If sugar is being used, the quantity of green gram dhal may be reduced by a handful and supplemented with a handful of Bengal gram dhal.

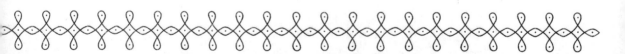

BROKEN WHEAT PONGAL

(GODHUMAI RAVA PONGAL)

The wheat should be coarsely broken. Steam the wheat with the water in a cooker or steamer. Cook over a slow flame. Add more water, if necessary, to cook the wheat. Keep turning it often so that it does not stick to the bottom of the vessel. When the wheat is cooked, remove from fire and strain out water completely.

Dry roast green gram dhal lightly. Wash well. Cook in 1½ to 2 cups water. When cooked, drain out the water.

Cut the ginger into small pieces. Heat the ghee in a frying pan. Fry the cashewnuts, broken pepper, cumin seeds and cut ginger. Add cooked wheat and dhal along with salt. Mix well. Take care to see the 'pongal' does not stick to the sides. Remove from fire and serve hot.

Ingredients

Broken wheat 2 cups

Water 4 cups

Green gram dhal ½ cup

Ghee 3-4 cups

Cashewnuts 12

Black peppercorns (Broken) 3-4 tsp

Cumin seeds 1 tsp

Ginger A marble-sized bit

Salt 1½ tsp

To serve 4 persons

IDLI

(WITH PAR-BOILED RICE)

Ingredients

Par-boiled rice 2½ cups
Raw rice ¼ cup
Black gram dhal 1 cup
Fenugreek seeds 1 tsp
(Optional)
Rock salt ¼ - ½ cup

To serve 4 persons

Wash the rice twice. Drain water. Soak the rice in 5 cups of fresh water for not less than 2 hours. Wash the dhal twice or thrice. Soak in 2 to 3 cups water separately for not less than 2 hours. The dhal may be soaked with fenugreek seeds.

Grind the rice into a somewhat rough and firm mass in a mixie/food processor, adding enough water. Grind the dhal separately, sprinkling a little water first, till it becomes smooth. Keep adding water, little by little, while grinding the dhal till it becomes very soft, very smooth and spongy. Remove and mix with the ground rice. Add salt. Mix the rice and dhal vigorously together. Transfer the dough to a large vessel, for as the dough ferments it increases in volume. If the container is too small, the dough will spill over the sides as it expands. Keep the lid tightly closed. Allow the dough to ferment for at least 24 hours.

Lightly grease the hollows in an idli tray with oil. Pour a little dough into each hollow. Do not fill the hollow completely as the idli expands while cooking. Boil water in a pressure cooker. Place the filled idli tray in it. Close the lid. Do not put on the 'weight'. Steam the idlis on a high fire. When the idlis are cooked, water will start dripping from the lid. It takes at least 10 minutes for the idlis to cook well. To check if the idlis are done, open the lid and insert a fork into one. If the dough does not

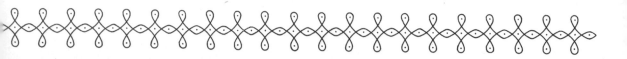

stick, it means that the idli is cooked. If the idlis are not fully cooked, steam for some more time. When cooked, take out the idli tray from the cooker. Sprinkle water round the idlis. Invert the idli trays to remove idlis. Serve hot with coconut chutney and sambar.

Note:

Even if the dhal is of an inferior quality, the idlis will still be soft if fenugreek seeds are used.

If the dough is allowed to ferment for too long, the idlis will taste sour. Thus on hot days, if idlis are to be prepared in the evening, the dough can be prepared in the morning, as it will not need 24 hours to ferment.

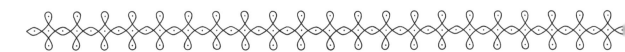

IDLI

(WITH RAW RICE)

Ingredients

Raw rice 2½ cups

Black gram dhal 1 cup

Fenugreek seeds 1 tsp
(Optional)

Rock salt ¼-½ cup

To serve 4 persons

Idlis can be prepared with raw rice as well if par-boiled rice is not available.

Wash and soak the rice for 2 to 3 hours. Wash again. Drain the water completely and powder the rice in a mill or mixie/food processor. Sift the rice powder through a coarse sieve. Knead the sieved rice flour into a firm dough with tepid water. Soak black gram dhal and fenugreek seeds, if being used, for 2 to 3 hours. Grind dhal into a very smooth spongy mass, adding water a little at a time while grinding. Mix with the rice dough along with the salt. Allow the dough to ferment for at least 24 hours before preparing idlis. (See pp. 54-55 on how to prepare the idlis.)

Note:

Pinched curry leaves or a little bit of dried ginger ('sukku') may be mixed with the dough.

If the dough is allowed to ferment for too long, the idlis will taste sour. Thus on hot days, if idlis are to be prepared in the evening, the dough can be prepared in the morning, as it will not need 24 hours to ferment.

SEMOLINA IDLI
(RAVA IDLI)

Heat ghee in a frying pan and fry the semolina till it turns light brown in colour. Keep aside. Chop green chillies and ginger. Heat 2 tsp of ghee in a frying pan and fry the mustard, green chillies and ginger. Break the cashewnuts into small bits and fry in ghee. Mix the seasonings and fried semolina with the sour curd. Add salt.

Boil water in a idli vessel. Cover the hollows of an idli tray with bits of plantain leaf. When the water has boiled, pour out the semolina mixture into the hollows. (If necessary, add water to the semolina mixture so that it can be easily poured.) When the water boils, insert the idli tray into the vessel and steam the idlis. When cooked remove from the tray on to a plate. Repeat till all the mixture is used up.

Note:
Add enough water to the semolina mixture only at the time of pouring out the idlis to prevent them from becoming sticky.

Ingredients

Semolina 2 cups
Ghee ¼ cup
Green chillies 4-5
Ginger ½"-1" piece
Mustard seeds 1 tsp
Cashewnuts 12
Curd (Sour) 1 cup
Salt 1 tsp

To serve 4 persons

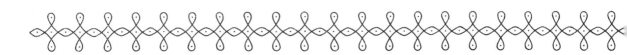

DOSAI

Ingredients

Par-boiled rice *3 cups*
Raw rice *1/4 cup*
Black gram dhal *1 cup*
Fenugreek seeds *1 tsp*
Rock salt *1/4 cup*
Oil *As required*

To serve *4 persons*

Wash the par-boiled and raw rice well and keep soaked in water for at least 2 to 3 hours. Wash the black gram dhal well and soak along with fenugreek seeds, also for 2 to 3 hours. Grind the rice into a smooth, firm paste. Separately grind the dhal into a smooth spongy mass. Mix both together with salt.

If you want to prepare the dosais immediately, mix 1/2 cup of sour buttermilk with the batter. Otherwise, allow the dough to ferment for 24 hours as for idlis. If the dosai batter is to be used on the same day, do not use fenugreek seeds. If it is to be kept for more than 24 hours, first grind the rice separately. The next morning, grind the dhal and fenugreek seeds together, mix with the rice paste and prepare the dosais in the evening. This will make the dosais tasty and not too sour. Mix enough water to the fermented dough to prepare a semi-solid batter.

Heat a flat pan or 'tava' on a low flame. (The 'tava' should not be concave.) Pour 1 tsp of oil on it and smear it all over with a soft, clean rag. Pour another 1/2 tsp in the centre. Pour about 1/5 cup (or a large ladle) of the batter on to the pan and spread into a circle. Cook over a slow fire. Use a flat ladle to scrape the sides and centre of the dosai before flipping the side. Spread a little oil on the side now facing down and cook. When both sides are well cooked, remove from the 'tava' on to a

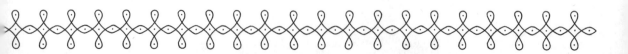

plate. Continue till all the batter is used up. Before preparing each dosai, remember to smear a little oil on the 'tava' before spreading the dosai.

Note:

If the dhal is of a very good quality or if you found that the dosais tended to stick to the pan when preparing, then use only 3/4 cup of black gram dhal for every 3 cups of par-boiled rice.

Add water to the fermented dough in batches to make the semi-solid batter.

Dip the flat ladle used to flip the dosai in a small vessel filled with water. Clean it each time before using.

Nowadays, non-stick 'dosai tavas' are available which can be used.

WHEAT DOSAI
(GODHUMAI DOSAI)

Ingredients

Wheat flour *1 cup*

Rice flour *1 cup*

Salt *2 tsp*

Buttermilk *(Sour) ½ cup*

Ginger *1"-2" piece*

Green chillies *2-3*

Cumin seeds *½ tsp*

Asafoetida water *1 tsp*

Curry leaves *(Broken) 2-3 tbsp*

Oil or ghee *As required*

To serve *4 persons*

Mix the wheat flour and rice flour together with the salt in the buttermilk. Add enough water to prepare a batter the consistency of thick buttermilk. Chop the ginger and green chillies. Mix the cumin seeds, asafoetida water, curry leaves and chopped ginger and green chillies in the batter. Allow the batter to stand for about 2 hours.

Heat a flat pan or 'tava' on a low flame. Smear 1 tsp of oil with a soft rag on the 'tava'. Pour 1/5 cup of batter on the 'tava' and spread into a circle. When the dosai cooks, small holes will appear on the surface. Pour 1 tsp of oil around the dosai and 1 tsp on the surface. Continue to cook over a low flame. When the side facing downwards turns golden, flip the dosai and cook till the other side also turns golden. If necessary, use more oil to cook the dosai. When ready, slide off on to a plate. Continue till all the batter is used up.

Note:

The dosais can also be prepared with a mixture of refined wheat flour and rice flour (in equal quantities).

A mixture of ghee and oil can be used to enhance the flavour.

Chopped onions can replace cumin seeds for variety.

Mix the batter well before preparing the dosais as the water will rise to the top when the batter is left to stand.

SEMOLINA DOSAI
(RAVA DOSAI)

Mix the semolina, rice flour and salt in the buttermilk
along with water and prepare a batter. Allow the batter
to stand for at least 2 hours. The semolina should soak
well, otherwise the dosais will stick to the pan.
Preferably, to prepare dosais in the morning, prepare the
batter the previous evening. If the dosais are to be
prepared in the evening, prepare the batter that morning.

Cut the ginger and green chillies. Add along with the
mustard and curry leaves to the batter just before
preparing the dosais.

Cook the dosais like the wheat dosais (see p. 60).
Use a mixture of ghee and oil when cooking rava
dosais. Oil will need to be used liberally as the dosais
should be crisp.

Note:
Ragi flour, maize or corn flour, or rice flour—all soaked
separately—can be used as well to prepare dosais.

A mixture of rice flour, refined wheat flour (maida) and
semolina (2 cups, 1 cup and 1/2 cup respectively) can
also be used.

Ingredients

Semolina 2 cups
Rice flour 1/4 cup
Salt 1 1/2 tsp
Buttermilk (Sour) 1/2 cup
Ginger 1"-2"piece
Green chillies 2-3
Mustard seeds 1 tsp
Curry leaves (Broken) 2-3
tbsp
Oil or ghee As required

To serve 4 persons

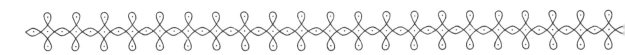

WHEAT FLOUR JAGGERY DOSAI
(GODHUMAI VELLA DOSAI)

Ingredients

Jaggery (Powdered) ¾-1 cup
Water 2 cups
Wheat flour 2 cups
Rice flour ¼ cup
Coconut ¼-½ (Medium)
Green cardamoms 5-6
Oil, ghee or vanaspati As required

To serve 4 persons

Heat the water and dissolve the jaggery in it. Remove from fire and let it become lukewarm. Add the wheat flour and rice flour. Mix well, taking care to break all the lumps. Grate coconut finely and add. Powder cardamom and mix.

Heat a flat pan or 'tava'. Smear it with 1 tsp of oil. Take ⅕ cup of the batter and spread on the pan as a thick cake. Pour oil around it and on top. When the base is cooked to a reddish brown colour, turn it slowly with a flat ladle. Pour 1 tsp of ghee or vanaspati on top and around. Remove when the other side is cooked as well. Cook the dosai over a low flame otherwise it will get scorched due to the jaggery.

Note:
Wheat flour can be replaced with maize flour or ragi flour.

OOTHAPPAM

Soak the rice for 2 to 3 hours. Separately soak the red gram dhal with the fenugreek seeds also for 2 to 3 hours. Wash the soaked rice and dhal. Grind the rice into a rough paste. (Not as rough as the idli batter but not as smooth as for dosais either.) Grind the dhal and fenugreek seeds together into a soft spongy mass. Mix with the rice dough along with the salt. Keep overnight. Prepare the oothappams the next day.

Heat a flat pan or 'tava'. Smear 1 tsp of oil and pour out 1/5 cup of batter. Spread into a thick round cake. Turn and cook both sides to a reddish brown, adding another spoon of oil.

Note:

If you want to use only 1 cup of rice, then soak all the ingredients together (i.e., rice, 1/2 cup red gram dhal and 1/2 tbsp fenugreek seeds). Grind together. Add salt and mix.

Raw rice may be used as well. For 1 1/2 cups of raw rice, use 1 cup of red gram dhal. But oothappams prepared with raw rice are not as tasty as those prepared with par- boiled rice.

Chopped onions or tomatoes or both can be sprinkled on one side for variety.

Ingredients

Par-boiled rice 2 cups
Red gram dhal 1 cup
Fenugreek seeds 1 tbsp
Salt 1/4 cup
Oil As required

To serve 4 persons

Photograph on p. 64

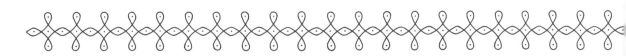

ADAI

Ingredients

Par-boiled rice *2 cups*

Red gram dhal *⅓ cup*

Bengal gram dhal *⅓ cup*

Black gram dhal *⅓ cup*

Salt *¼ cup*

Dry red chillies *5-6*

Green chillies *8-10*

Asafoetida powder *A pinch or to taste*

Coconut *½ (Medium)*

Coriander leaves *3-4 tbsp*

Curry leaves *12-15*

Ginger *1"-2" piece*

Oil *As required*

To serve *4 persons*

Wash the rice and the three dhals. Soak altogether for at least 2 to 3 hours. Grind into a rough paste-like dough with the salt, red chillies, five or six green chillies (whole) and asafoetida. (The paste should be as coarse a mixture as that of semolina and water.)

Grate coconut. Pinch coriander leaves and curry leaves. Chop ginger and remaining green chillies. Mix grated coconut, coriander and curry leaves, and chopped ginger and green chillies into the ground paste.

Heat a flat pan or 'tava'. Smear the heated pan with 1 tsp of oil all over. Pour 1/5 cup of dough in the centre. Draw it into a circle, either with your hand or a flat ladle. The 'adai' should not be very thin. Make a small hole in the middle of the 'adai' with a spoon. Pour 1 tsp of oil right round. Pour another spoon of oil into the hole in the centre and over the 'adai'. When one side turns golden brown, turn and toss and cook the other side, pouring 1 tsp of oil. Remove from fire and serve hot. Continue till all the batter is used up.

Note:

Finely chopped onions, drumstick leaves, cabbage, cauliflower or cucumber may be mixed with the dough. When onions are used, it is not necessary to use coconut.

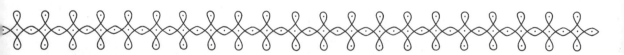

'Adais' can be made with raw rice as well. If raw rice is being used, grind it in a mill. The rice flour should have the coarseness of semolina. Knead into dough with tepid water. For 2 cups of rice flour, soak and grind 1 cup of the three dhals combined. Grind the dhals with salt, chillies and asafoetida. Knead the ground dhals into the rice dough and prepare into 'adai'.

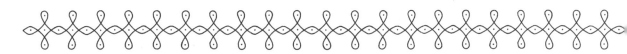

JAGGERY ADAI

Ingredients

Coconut ½ (Medium)
Green cardamoms 10-12
Lentil beans ½-¾ cup
Jaggery 4 cups
Water 10 cups
Rice flour (Roasted) 4 cups

To serve 4 persons

Cut the coconut into fine little bits. Powder cardamom. Roast the lentil beans a little and cook in water. Drain any excess water. Powder the jaggery. Heat the water in a wide mouthed vessel. Add the jaggery and boil. When the jaggery is completely dissolved and the water boils vigorously, pour in the rice flour and stir continuously. Add cooked lentil beans and coconut. When the flour is half-cooked and becomes a mass, remove from fire. Mix cardamom powder. (Cooked lentil beans and coconut may be added at this stage also.)

Spread a greased plantain leaf over a single idli tray. Take a little of the cooked flour and flatten it out with your palm like a thick 'vadai' (¼ inch thick). Make a hole in the centre. Arrange on the tray. Boil water in a pan or pressure cooker. Insert the single idli tray. Close the lid. Steam and cook the 'adais' for about 10 minutes. When the 'adais' are cooked, remove from tray on to a plate. (To check if the 'adais' have cooked, insert a fork into one. If the batter does not stick, then the 'adais' are cooked.) Continue till all the batter is used up. Serve hot with butter.

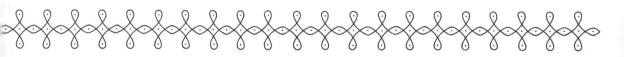

PESARAT

(GREEN GRAM DHAL DOSAI)

Wash rice and dhal. Soak together for 2 to 3 hours.
Strain the water. Grind to a paste adding salt, green
chillies and ginger. The batter should be of a medium
consistency like that prepared for oothappams. Set the
batter aside to ferment for at least 8 hours. If you want
to prepare the dosai immediately, add the sour
buttermilk. Take care not to make the batter too watery.

Heat a flat pan or 'tava'. Grease the 'tava' with 1 tsp oil.
Mix the batter well and pour 1/5 cup of batter on to the
pan. Spread the batter in a circular motion to make a
round dosai. Pour 1-1½ tsp of oil around and over the
dosai. Cook till one side turns golden brown. Flip and
cook the other side, pouring another teaspoon of oil
around and over the dosai. Remove from fire and
serve hot.

Note:
A little asafoetida water, mustard seasoning (½ tsp) and
pinched curry leaves may also be added to the batter
before preparing the dosais.

Ingredients

Green gram dhal 2 cups
Rice ¼ cup
Salt 2 tsp
Green chillies 6-8
Ginger 1" piece
Buttermilk (Sour) ¼ cup
(Optional)
Oil As required

To serve 4 persons

POORI

Ingredients

Wheat flour 2 cups
Ghee or vanaspati For frying

To serve 4 persons

Knead the flour with 2-3 tsp ghee and enough water into a soft, but not loose, dough. It is not necessary to let it stand for a long time.

Pinch and roll the dough into small balls. Keep some flour on a plate. Dip the balls in it and roll into thick rounds with a rolling pin.

Heat enough ghee or vanaspati in a deep frying pan. Fry pooris while still damp. Cook both sides, turning with a flat spoon. (Do not let the pooris turn crisp.) Remove from fire. Drain the oil and serve hot with masala potato. (See recipe on p. 31.)

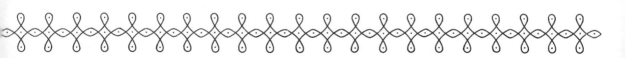

SEMOLINA UPPUMA

(RAVA UPPUMA)

Sift the semolina. Roast in a pan to a light golden colour. Keep aside. Chop the ginger and keep aside.

Heat the oil and ghee in a frying pan. Season with mustard, black gram dhal, cashewnuts, pinched red chillies and asafoetida. Add the chopped ginger, whole green chillies and curry leaves. Fry a little and pour in the water. Add salt. When the water boils vigorously, add the semolina and go on stirring to prevent lumps. When the water is absorbed and the semolina cooked, remove from fire. The 'uppuma' should not be a mass but soft and powdery.

Note:

If the semolina is of very good quality, it can be added after the seasoning and fried till golden brown. Then add the water and salt, mix well and cook.

If semolina is of a very fine variety, decrease the quantity of water.

The juice of half a lime can be added after removing the 'uppuma' from the fire. Mix well and serve. Alternatively, 1/2 cup sour buttermilk can also be added after removing the 'uppuma' from the fire. If using buttermilk, reduce the quantity of water by 1/2 cup.

Ingredients

Semolina 2 cups
Ginger 1" piece
Oil 4-5 tsp
Ghee 3 tsp
Mustard seeds 1 tsp
Black gram dhal 2 tsp
Cashewnuts 7-8
Dry red chillies 2-3
Asafoetida powder A pinch
or to taste
Green chillies 2-3
Curry leaves 8-10
Water 3 cups
Salt 1 1/2 tsp

To serve 4 persons

RICE UPPUMA

(ARISI UPPUMA)

Ingredients

Rice *2 cups*

Red gram dhal *¼ cup*

Coconut *¼ (Medium)*

Gingelly oil or coconut oil
7-8 tsp

Mustard seeds *1 tsp*

Black gram dhal *2 tsp*

Dry red chillies *4-5*

Asafoetida powder *A pinch
or to taste*

Water *3 cups*

Salt *1½ tsp*

Curry leaves *8-10*

To serve *4 persons*

Coarsely powder the rice and dhal (preferably in a machine mill or in a mixie/food processor). Sieve and keep aside. Grate coconut.

Heat a large enough vessel which can cook 2 cups of rice. Pour the oil in it. Fry mustard, black gram dhal, pinched red chillies and asafoetida. Pour in the water. Add salt, grated coconut and pinched curry leaves. Cover with a lid. When the water boils vigorously, add the sieved rice and dhal powder, turning all the while with a ladle. Cover the vessel, placing a small bowl containing water on the lid. If the water boiled initially is not enough to cook the rice, add a little water from this bowl. Cook the rice over a slow fire, turning quite often. Remove from fire. Turn well twice or three times and serve.

Note:

Cumin seeds and broken black peppercorns can be added to the seasonings. This will give the 'uppuma' the flavour of pongal. Cashewnuts and Bengal gram dhal are also options that can be added to the seasoning.

BROKEN WHEAT UPPUMA

(GODHUMAI RAVA UPPUMA)

Chop the ginger and keep aside. Heat the oil and ghee in a frying pan. Fry mustard, black gram dhal, cashewnuts, pinched red chillies and asafoetida. Add the chopped ginger, whole green chillies and curry leaves. Fry a little and add the broken wheat. Pour in the water. Add salt. Go on stirring to prevent lumps. When the water is absorbed and the wheat cooked, remove from fire. Serve hot.

Ingredients

Ginger *1" piece*

Oil *4-5 tsp*

Ghee *3 tsp*

Mustard *1 tsp*

Black gram dhal *2 tsp*

Cashewnuts *7 8*

Dry red chillies *2*

Asafoetida powder *A pinch or to taste*

Green chillies *2*

Curry leaves *8-10*

Broken wheat *2 cups*

Water *2½ cups*

Salt *1 tsp*

To serve *4 persons*

VERMICELLI UPPUMA

(SEMIA UPPUMA)

Ingredients

Ginger ½" piece
Vermicelli 450 gms
Ghee 3 tbsp
Oil 4-5 tbsp
Mustard seeds 1 tbsp
Black gram dhal 1 tsp
Cashewnuts 30 gms
Dry red chillies 2
Curry leaves 8-10
Water 3 cups
Salt 1½ tsp

To serve 4 persons

Photograph on p. 63

Chop ginger and keep aside. Fry the vermicelli till golden brown in 1 tbsp ghee. Keep aside. In the same pan, add a little more ghee and oil and heat. Add mustard, black gram dhal, cashewnuts, pinched red chillies, chopped ginger and pinched curry leaves. Fry as for semolina 'uppuma'. Add water and salt to the seasonings. Boil vigorously. Add the vermicelli. Cook, turning it all the while. A little more water can be added, if the quantity of water is not enough. See that the 'uppuma' does not become very soft or lumpy. When water is absorbed, remove from fire. Serve hot.

Note:
The juice of half a lime can be added after removing the 'uppuma' from the fire. Alternatively, 1/2 cup sour buttermilk can also be added after removing the 'uppuma' from the fire. If using buttermilk, reduce the quantity of water by 1/2 cup. Mix well and serve.

Chopped onions may also be added. Add onions after the seasonings and fry well before adding water. If onions are used, lime juice must also be added, to enhance the taste.

If more water is required to cook the 'uppuma', do not pour the entire quantity in one go, as the 'uppuma' will turn lumpy. Sprinkle the water, a little at a time, mix well and cook. Stop when the water is enough.

TAMARIND FLAVOURED BEATEN RICE FLAKES
(PULI AVAL)

Clean beaten rice flakes. Crush and wash. Soak the tamarind and prepare 1 cup of thick juice. Mix tamarind juice with washed beaten rice flakes. Add salt and turmeric powder and mix well. Let stand for 10 minutes.

Heat oil in a frying pan. Fry the mustard, Bengal gram dhal, black gram dhal, asafoetida powder and pinched red chillies. Chop the green chillies and add. Fry well. Add the beaten rice flakes soaked in tamarind and pinched curry leaves. Fry till dry and serve hot.

Ingredients

Beaten rice flakes *2 cups*
Tamarind *A lump the size of a lime*
Salt *1½ tsp*
Turmeric powder *¼ tsp*
Oil *7-8 tsp*
Mustard seeds *1 tsp*
Bengal gram dhal *2 tsp*
Black gram dhal *2 tsp*
Asafoetida powder *A pinch or to taste*
Dry red chillies *4-5*
Green chillies *4-5*
Curry leaves *5-6*

To serve *4 persons*

SEMIA BAHALA BATH
(VERMICELLI IN CURD)

Ingredients

Vermicelli *225 gms*
Ghee *4 tsp*
Water *1½ cups*
Salt *2 tsp*
Milk *¼ litre*
Curd *¼ litre*
Oil *2 tsp*
Mustard seeds *1 tsp*
Green chillies *4-5*
Ginger *½"-1" piece*
Asafoetida *A pinch or to taste*
Curry leaves *5-6*
Coriander leaves *2 tbsp*

To serve *4 persons*

Heat the ghee in a frying pan and fry vermicelli till golden brown. Add water and 1 tsp salt and cook. When well cooked, remove from fire. Cool. Mix in the milk and curd (the curd should be sweet and firm) and the remaining spoon of salt.

Heat oil in a frying pan. Add mustard, chopped green chillies and chopped ginger. Prepare asafoetida water and add along with fresh curry leaves and coriander leaves. Mix well and serve.

Note:

Cashewnuts, fried in ghee, may also be added.

A little butter also imparts a very good taste.

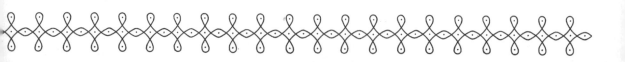

VADAI
(ULUNDHU VADAI)

Soak the black gram dhal in 4-5 cups water for an hour
or two. Wash and clean well. Drain excess water. Grind
into a smooth dough in a mixie/food processor with the
salt. Chop green chillies and ginger. Add to the dough.
Pinch curry leaves (into fine pieces) and mix with the
dough. The vadais can be prepared immediately.

Heat the oil in a frying pan. Wet a piece of plantain leaf.
Place a little dough on it and flatten it out into a circle
(the vadai should not be too thick). Make a little hole in
the centre with your little finger. Slide into the oil. Fry
four to five vadais at a time in hot oil, turning gently
with a flat spoon. Cook both sides to a reddish brown.
Drain out the oil and serve. Continue to fry the vadais
in batches till all the dough is used up.

Note:
Four or five red chillies may be ground with the dhal if
vadais are preferred chilli hot.

Ingredients

Black gram dhal 2 cups
Salt 2 tsp
Green chillies 7-8
Ginger 2" piece
Curry leaves 8-10
Oil 3 cups

To serve 4 persons

CURD VADAI

(THAYIR VADAI)

Ingredients

Black gram dhal 1 cup

Red gram dhal 1 cup

Salt 2 tsp

Green chillies 12

Asafoetida A pinch or to taste

Curry leaves 8-10

Coriander leaves 2 tbsp

Curd 2 cups

Milk ½ cup

Coconut ½ (Medium)

Ginger A small bit

Oil 2-3 cups

Mustard 1 tsp

To serve 4 persons

Photograph on p. 81

Soak the dhals together for 2 hours. Wash and drain. Grind to a very smooth dough with 1 tsp salt, five or six green chillies and asafoetida. Pinch the curry leaves and 1 tbsp coriander leaves and mix into the dough. The dough can be used immediately to prepare the vadais.

The curd used for this dish must be sweet and firm. Mix the curd and milk together with 1 tsp salt. Grate the coconut. Grind to a very fine smooth paste along with the remaining coriander leaves, four green chillies and ginger. Mix the paste with the curd. Chop two green chillies. Heat 2 tsp oil in a frying pan. Fry the mustard and chopped green chillies. Season the curd.

Fry the vadais in batches. (See Vadai recipe on p. 77.) Cook till golden brown turning gently with a perforated spoon. Do not make holes in the centre of the vadai. Remove from oil. Press the vadais to drip out the oil and drop into the seasoned curd. Continue to fry the vadais in batches and soak in the curd till all the dough is used up. Soak each batch in the curd for 2 to 3 hours. The earlier soaked ones can be removed to a plate before dipping the fresh ones, if necessary. Pour any remaining curd over the vadais before serving.

Note:
If the seasoned curd becomes very firm, add milk or more curd, according to taste.

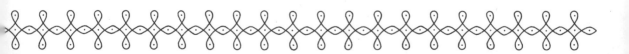

Kara Vadai

Soak black gram dhal for 2 hours and grind. (The consistency of the dough should be like for idlis.) Allow dough to stand for at least 8 hours. Soak Bengal gram dhal separately for 2 hours. Wash and drain well. Mix black gram dhal batter, rice flour, Bengal gram flour, salt, chilli powder and the soaked Bengal gram dhal. Mix well into a thick dough, adding the asafoetida water. Add chopped ginger and green chillies. Heat 2 tsp oil in a frying pan. Fry mustard and curry leaves and season the batter.

Heat the oil in a deep frying pan. Take a handful of dough. Roll into small balls and drop in the oil. Cook for a while. Prick with a fork in a couple of places. Turn gently and cook till crisp. The vadais should be crisp on the outside and soft inside. Drain oil and serve hot.

Note:

If you want to prepare the vadais immediately, add the sour curd. If vadais are to be prepared in the evening, grind the black gram dhal in the morning and add the other ingredients to the dough just before frying.

Ingredients

Black gram dhal ½ cup
Bengal gram dhal ¼ cup
Raw rice flour 1½ cups
Bengal gram flour ½ cup
Salt 2 tsp
Chilli powder 2 tsp
Asafoetida water 1 tsp
Ginger 1" piece
Green chillies 5-6
Oil 2-3 cups
Mustard seeds 1 tsp
Curry leaves 8-10
Curd (Sour) ⅓ cup (Optional)

To serve 4 persons

MYSORE BONDA

Ingredients

Black gram dhal *2 cups*

Salt *2 tsp*

Green chillies *7-8*

Ginger *1" piece*

Coconut *¼ (Medium)*

Curry leaves *8-10*

Coriander leaves *2-3 tbsp*

Oil *2-3 cups*

Mustard seeds *1 tsp*

To serve *4 persons*

Soak the black gram dhal for 2 hours. Wash and grind into a smooth, spongy dough, along with salt. The dough should be firm and thick. Finely chop green chillies, ginger and coconut. Mix with the dough. Add pinched curry leaves and coriander leaves. Heat 1 tsp oil in a frying pan and fry the mustard. Season the dough with the fried mustard.

Heat the oil in a frying pan. Keep a little water separately in a vessel. Wet your hand in the water. Take a small lime size ball of the dough and drop it into the oil. (Do not roll the dough too much.) Cook to a reddish brown colour, turning gently with a flat spoon. Remove from fire, drain the oil and serve. Cook about four to eight bondas at a time. Continue to fry in batches till all the dough is used up.

POTATO BONDA

Boil the potatoes. Peel and mash. Add salt and turmeric powder. Extract juice from the lime and mix with the mashed potatoes. Chop green chillies and ginger. Heat oil in a frying pan. Fry mustard. Add ginger and green chillies and fry a little. Add mashed potatoes. Add asafoetida water and pinched coriander and curry leaves. Mix well. Remove from fire. When cool, roll into small arecanut size balls.

Mix all the ingredients for the batter with enough water to make a thick batter. Dip each potato ball into the batter, coating it evenly on all sides.

Heat enough oil in a deep frying pan. Drop the bondas in the hot oil and cook to a reddish brown colour, turning gently. Remove from fire. Serve hot.

Note:
Cashewnuts (about twenty) broken into small bits and fried till golden can be added to the filling mixture.

Finely chopped onions too may be included. Peel and chop onions and fry with the seasonings.

Ingredients for the filling

Potato 350 gms
Salt 1 tsp
Turmeric powder ½ tsp
Lime 1
Green chillies 4
Ginger 1" piece
Oil 2-3 tsp
Mustard seeds 1 tsp
Asafoetida water ½ tsp
Coriander leaves 2 tbsp
Curry leaves 8-10

Ingredients for the batter

Bengal gram dhal flour 1½ cups
Rice flour ½ cup
Salt ¼ tsp
Chilli powder 2 tsp
Baking soda A pinch
Asafoetida powder A pinch or to taste
Oil (for frying) 2-3 cups

To serve 4 persons

BAJJI

(PAKORAS)

Ingredients

Bengal gram dhal flour ½ cup

Rice flour 1 cup

Refined wheat flour (Maida) ½ cup

Salt 2 tsp

Baking soda A pinch

Chilli powder 2½-3 tsp

Asafoetida A pinch or to taste

Curd (Sour) ⅕ cup

Vegetable 100-150 gms

Oil 3 cups

To serve 4 persons

Mix Bengal gram dhal flour, rice flour and refined wheat flour together. Add salt, baking soda and chilli powder. Prepare asafoetida water and mix with the curd. Add to the flour and prepare a thick batter with enough water.

The following vegetables may be used: brinjal, plantain, Bangalore brinjal, potato, snake gourd, pumpkin and ridge gourd. If you are using ridge gourd, plantain or Bangalore brinjal, scrape the skin off first and then cut into thin long slices. Cut other vegetables into thin rings.

Heat oil in a deep frying pan. Dip the cut vegetable in the batter. Cover both sides well. Drop the batter-covered vegetables into the oil. Fry till golden brown. Drain oil and serve hot. Continue to fry in batches.

Note:

If the snake gourd is not tender, cut into thin bits, mix with 1/2 tsp salt, keep for a few minutes, squeeze out water, mix with the batter and fry as small balls. Small onions, cabbage leaves and amaranth leaves too may be shredded and mixed with the batter and 'bajjis' prepared. Tender amaranth leaves (after discarding the stems) should be sliced, washed and dipped in the batter and fried till reddish brown.

Left over dosai batter can also be used. Mix all the ingredients in the dosai batter. Do not use curd.

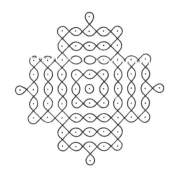

SAVOURIES

MURUKKU

Roast rice in a frying pan. (Do not let the colour change.)
When cool, wash and drain (pour through a bamboo
basket or colander). Grind into flour (in a mill or mixie/
food processor) and sift through a fine sieve. Do not let the
rice remain damp for a long time before grinding. Dry
roast black gram dhal to a reddish colour and grind into a
very smooth powder (in a mill or mixie/food processor).
Sift through a fine sieve. Dissolve asafoetida and salt in 1/4
cup water. Mix rice flour, black gram dhal flour, asafoetida
and salt water and cumin seeds. Knead with a little water.
Add butter or ghee and knead well into a firm dough.

Spread the dough on a white cloth. Dip fingers in coconut
oil. Take a little of the dough and spin out into circles,
giving the dough a twist. Make three or four rounds. Each
'murukku' will resemble a circle, made of rows of twisted
cord. Make all the dough into as many 'murukkus' as
possible. When half the dough has been made into
'murukkus', heat oil or vanaspati in a frying pan. Gently
slide four or five 'murukkus' into the hot oil, choosing the
ones that have become comparatively dry. (Take care not to
break the 'murukkus'.) When half-cooked, turn and cook
the other side, till both sides are golden brown and the
hissing sound ceases. Remove from fire and drain. When
cool, store in an airtight container.

Note:
Do not keep the dough for a long time, as the
'murukku' will turn red.

Ingredients

Rice 4 cups
Black gram dhal ½ cup
Asafoetida A pinch or to taste
Salt ½ cup
Cumin seeds 2 tsp
*Butter or firm ghee (for
kneading)* ½ cup
*Vanaspati or coconut oil
(for frying)* 1½ cups

Photograph on p. 82

BLACK GRAM DHAL THENKUZHAL
(ULUNDU THENKUZHAL)

Ingredients

Rice *4 cups*

Black gram dhal *1 cup*

Cumin seeds *2 tsp*

Asafoetida *A pinch or to taste*

Salt *¼-½ cup*

Ghee or butter *(for kneading)*
½ cup

Ghee or coconut oil *(for
frying) 2½ cups*

Wash rice. Soak for a while. Drain out and dry in the shade. Grind in a mill into a fine flour and sift. Roast the black gram dhal till it becomes hot. Grind in a mill. Sift and mix with the rice flour. Add cumin seeds. Mix asafoetida in water. Dissolve salt in water. Pour asafoetida water and salt water into the ground flour. Add the butter or ghee and enough water and knead into a firm dough.

Heat the ghee or coconut oil in a frying pan. Insert the perforated 'thenkuzhal disc' in the 'thenkuzhal' press. Put a little of the dough in the bottom part of the press. Holding the press over the oil, press out the 'thenkuzhal' with a circular motion of the hand, so that the 'thenkuzhal' is circular in shape. Make as many as can be fried without the 'thenkuzhal' touching one another. Cook one side till brown. Turn and cook the other side till the hissing sound ceases. Remove and drain excess oil. When cool, store in an airtight container. Fry in batches till all the dough is used up.

Note:
Raw rice and black gram dhal can be mixed and ground together in a machine.

Do not keep the dough for a long time, as the 'thenkuzhal' will turn red. So, divide the ingredients into two or three parts proportionately and mix the flour into dough in parts.

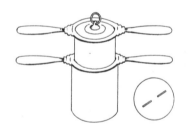

*Thenkuzhal Press
(with thenkuzhal disc)*

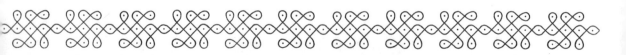

RIBBON THENKUZHAL

Mix the rice flour and Bengal gram dhal flour together.
Dissolve the salt in water. Pour into the mixed flour. Add
chilli powder and asafoetida water. Knead into a firm
dough with the ghee or butter, adding enough water.

Heat the oil in a frying pan. Insert the 'ribbon disc' in
the 'thenkuzhal' press. Put a little of the dough in the
bottom part of the press. Holding the press over the oil,
press out the ribbon 'thenkuzhal' into the hot oil. Cook
one side till brown and break the ribbons into
convenient lengths with a flat spoon. Turn and cook the
other side till the hissing sound ceases. Remove and
drain excess oil. When cool, store in an airtight
container. Fry in batches till all the dough is used up.

Ingredients

Rice flour 1 cup
Bengal gram dhal flour 2
cups
Salt 3 tsp
Chilli powder 3 tsp
Asafoetida water 1 tsp
Ghee or butter (for kneading)
1/5 cup
Oil (for frying) 2-3 cups

OMAPPODI

Ingredients

Rice flour 2 cups

Bengal gram dhal flour 4 cups

Salt 1/4 cup

Asafoetida water 1 tsp

Butter or firm ghee (for kneading) 1/3 cup

Ghee or coconut oil (for frying) 2-2½ cups

Mix 1 cup of rice flour with 2 cups of Bengal gram dhal flour. Add asafoetida water. Dissolve salt in 1/2 cup water. Add about 1/4 cup of salt water to the flour and knead into a dough with half the ghee or butter.

Insert the disc with the small holes in the 'thenkuzhal' press. Put a little of the dough in the bottom part of the press. Holding the press over the oil, press out the omapoddi into the hot oil in a circular motion. Cook one side. Turn and cook the other side till golden brown and the hissing sound ceases. When cooked, the omappodi rises to the top. Remove and drain excess oil. Prepare dough with the remaining ingredients and make omappodi till all the dough is used up. When cool, store in an airtight container.

Note:

You can also use Bengal gram flour and rice flour in equal quantities (i.e., 1 cup of rice flour and 1 cup of Bengal gram dhal flour).

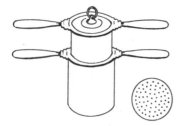

*Thenkuzhal Press
(with omappodi disc)*

KARA BOONDHI

Mix rice flour and Bengal gram dhal flour. Take half the quantity. Add half the baking soda, 1 tsp chilli powder and 1 tsp salt. Add 1-1¹/2 cups water. Pour asafoetida water over the flour and mix into a thick batter.

Insert the kara boondhi ('kunja ladu') disc. Pour out the batter into the press with a spoon and rub it through the holes with the bottom of the spoon while holding the press over the oil. Cook the boondhi into a fine gold colour, turning them often with a big spoon. Remove and drain excess oil. Mix the remaining ingredients and prepare boondhi till all the batter is used up. Fry the cashewnuts and the curry leaves separately. Mix with the prepared boondhi. When cool, store in an airtight container.

Note:
The boondhi can be prepared without using chilli powder. Use only salt and baking soda along with 2 tsp pepper.

You can also fry 7 or 8 red chillies with a little bit of asafoetida, powder them with salt and use it.

Ingredients

Bengal gram dhal flour 2 cups
Rice flour 1-2 cups
Baking soda ¹/4 tsp
Chilli powder 3 tsp
Salt 3 tsp
Asafoetida water 1 tsp
Vanaspati or coconut oil (for frying) 2-2¹/2 cups
Cashewnuts 20-40
Curry leaves 12-15

MIXTURE

Ingredients

Beaten rice flakes 150 gms

Bengal gram dhal 50-60 gms

Cashewnuts (Broken) 100 gms

Curry leaves 1/4 cup

Ghee or oil (for frying) 2-3 cups

Groundnuts 100 gms

Coconut 1/2 (Medium)

Asafoetida A pinch or to taste

Dry red chillies 8-10

Salt 1/4 cup

Omappodi 250 gms

Kara boondhi 100 gms

Sugar 2 tbsp

Ghee 1/4 cup

Refined wheat flour (Maida) 1-2 cups

Fry the beaten rice flakes, Bengal gram dhal, cashewnuts and curry leaves separately in ghee. Winnow the groundnuts and roast. Cut coconut into tiny little bits. Fry in ghee to a reddish colour. Fry asafoetida and red chillies. Powder fried red chillies with salt and asafoetida. Mix all the ingredients and the chilli-asafoetida powder together. Mix in kara boondhi (see recipe on p. 91) and omappodi (see recipe on p. 90). Dissolve the sugar in a little water. Mix 1/4 cup of ghee and the sugar solution with the refined wheat flour and knead into a dough. Roll out the dough in a circle on a floured board. Cut into small diamond sized bits and fry, adding them at the end to the 'mixture'.

Note:

Do not add coconut, if the mixture is to be kept for a long period.

Instead of fried Bengal gram dhal, roasted Bengal gram ('porikadalai') may be used (without husk), while it is still hot.

Potatoes cut into thin long bits and fried can also be added.

Instead of frying the beaten rice flakes, dry roast the flakes with sand in a pan. Sift out the sand and use the puffed flakes.

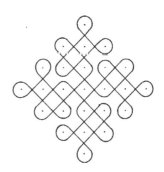

SWEETS

VERMICELLI PAYASAM

(SEMIA PAYASAM)

Heat ghee in a frying pan. Fry vermicelli till reddish brown. Fry cashewnuts separately.

In another vessel, boil the water. Add the fried vermicelli. Stir and cook till soft. Test by pressing the vermicelli between the fingers. When soft, add sugar. Let it mix well. Add milk along with the fried cashewnuts, cardamom, saffron and borneal flakes. Serve hot.

Note:

One-fourth of a nutmeg, fried and powdered, can also be added.

Ingredients

Ghee ¼ *cup*
Vermicelli 175 *gms*
Cashewnuts 15-20
Water 2 *cups*
Sugar 1½ *cups*
Milk 2 *cups*
Green cardamoms 7-8
Saffron ¼ *tsp*
Borneal flakes ¼ *tsp*

To serve 4 *persons*

GREEN GRAM DHAL PAYASAM

(PAYATHAM PARAPPU PAYASAM)

Ingredients

Green cardamoms 7-8
Ghee 1 tbsp
Cashewnuts 20
Green gram dhal 3/4 cup
Water 2 cups
Jaggery 1 cup
Milk or coconut milk 1 cup

To serve 4 persons

Powder the cardamoms. Heat ghee in a frying pan and fry cashewnuts till golden brown. Dry roast the dhal lightly. Wash four or five times.

Boil the water in a vessel. Add washed and roasted dhal. When dhal breaks up and mixes well with the water, add the jaggery. Let It melt completely. Add milk or coconut milk and remove from fire. (If coconut milk is being used, heat for a few seconds before removing from fire.) Add fried cashewnuts and cardamom powder and serve.

Note:

Instead of using only green gram dhal, 1/3 cup green gram dhal, 1/4 cup broken rice and 1/8 cup Bengal gram dhal may be used to make the payasam the same way.

Sago Payasam

(JAVVARISI PAYASAM)

Powder the cardamoms. Fry the cashewnuts in 2 tsp ghee till golden brown. Keep aside.

Heat a frying pan. Add the remaining ghee. Fry the sago till reddish brown. Add water and stir. Keep stirring to avoid lumps. Cook the sago till it swells, becomes transparent and very soft. Add the sugar and mix well. Pour in the milk. Add powdered cardamom, saffron and borneal flakes. Mix well and bring to boil. Add fried cashewnuts and serve hot.

Note:

Raw sago may be added to boiling water or raw sago mixed with cold water and then brought to boil, and the payasam prepared. Fried sago has a bitter flavour but is less sticky.

Ingredients

Green cardamoms 5-6
Cashewnuts 12
Ghee 4 tsp
Sago 3½ tbsp
Water 1½ cups
Sugar ½ cup
Milk 1 cup
Saffron ¼ tsp
Borneal flakes ¼-½ tsp

To serve 4 persons

ALMOND PAYASAM
(BADAM KHEER)

Ingredients

Ghee 4 tsp
Cashewnut (Broken) 1 tbsp
Pistachio 1 tbsp
Almonds (Shelled) 100 gms
Milk 2-3 cups
Sugar 1 cup
Green cardamoms 7-8
Borneal flakes 1/2 tsp
Saffron 1/4-1/2 tsp

To serve 4 persons

Photograph on p. 99

Heat ghee. Fry cashewnuts and pistachios till light brown. Keep aside. Soak the almonds in 1/2 cup warm water for an hour. Remove the skin and grind into a very smooth paste. Mix the paste with 2-3 cups of water and the milk. Bring the mixture to boil, stirring frequently, until you get the aroma of almonds. Add the sugar and mix well. Stir till sugar dissolves. Add the fried cashewnuts, pistachios, the cardamom, borneal flakes and saffron. Serve chilled.

Semolina Halwa

(RAVA KESARI)

Fry cashewnuts in 2 tsp ghee till golden brown and keep aside. Powder the cardamom. Fry the semolina in 2 tbsp ghee till golden brown. Add 2 1/2 to 3 cups of water (i.e., as much as necessary, depending on the quality of the semolina used). Stir well and cook. When the semolina is soft and has thickened slightly, add the sugar. The mixture will turn watery on adding sugar and will thicken on further cooking. After it thickens, add the rest of the ghee. Cook till the halwa forms a ball and leaves the sides of the pan. Remove from fire. Add cardamom powder and borneal flakes. Mix saffron soaked in 1-2 tbsp milk. Serve hot.

Ingredients

Cashewnuts 7-8
Ghee 1-1 1/2 cups
Green cardamoms 7-8
Semolina 2 cups
Water 2 1/2-3 cups
Sugar 2 1/2 cups
Borneal flakes 1/4 tsp
Saffron 1/4-1/2 tsp

To serve 4 persons

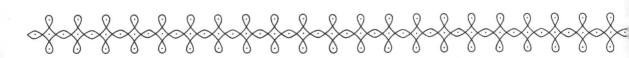

Wheat Halwa

(GODHUMAI HALWA)

Ingredients

White (or round) wheat
2 cups

Almonds *(Shelled) 100 gms*

Cashewnuts *30*

Ghee *2 cups*

Sugar *2 2½ cups*

Saffron *½-¾ tsp*

Green cardamom powder
½-1 tsp

Borneal flakes *¼-½ tsp*

To serve *4 persons*

Soak wheat in 5-6 cups water overnight. Grind the next morning, adding water little by little. Squeeze out milk at least three times. Filter through a sieve. Allow to stand without disturbing and decant and discard the clear water that rises to the top.

Soak almonds and peel. Grind roughly. Break cashewnuts into bits and fry in a little ghee till they turn reddish brown. In a vessel, add 2 to 2½ cups of sugar and ½ to ¾ cup of water. Stir over heat till sugar has dissolved. Boil rapidly until the syrup attains thread consistency.

Add the ground almonds to the wheat milk. Pour into the sugar syrup and continue stirring. Dissolve saffron in 1 tsp milk. When the milk and sugar mixture begins to thicken, add the saffron to the halwa. Add the ghee, little by little. Add fried cashewnuts. Go on stirring till the halwa hardens and forms a ball, leaving the sides of the vessel. Add cardamom powder and borneal flakes and mix. Remove from fire and serve hot.

Note:
The wheat milk should neither be thick nor too thin, but should be a semi-solid liquid.

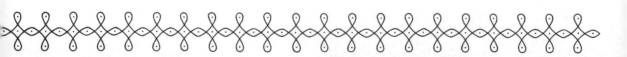

Mango Fruit Halwa

(MAMPAZHAM HALWA)

To make mango pulp, take well-ripe mangoes that are sweet as well as slightly sour and fibreless. Peel and squeeze out enough mangoes to prepare 4 cups of pulp. Mix the pulp well till there are no lumps. Put the mango pulp in a wide mouth heavy (e.g., bronze) vessel and place on fire. Mash it well with a ladle and stir. As soon as the pulp starts boiling, add the sugar and stir continuously. Fry the cashewnuts (broken into bits) in a little ghee. Add the fried cashewnuts to the boiling mango pulp and stir.

When the mango pulp has become thick, add the ghee little by little, stirring continuously. When the halwa starts leaving the sides of the vessel, remove from fire. Powder the cardamoms. Add cardamom powder and borneal flakes and mix well. Pour the halwa on a greased plate and when it cools, cut into pieces and serve.

Ingredients

Mango pulp 4 *cups*
Sugar 2 *cups*
Cashewnuts 35 *gms*
Ghee 200 *gms*
Green cardamoms 8
Borneal flakes A *pinch*

To serve 4 *persons*

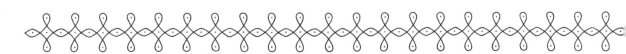

JANGIRI

Ingredients

Rice ¼ cup

Black gram dhal 2 cups

Sugar 10 cups

Water 4 cups

Milk ¼ cup

Rose essence 10-12 drops

Saffron ¼-½ tsp

Ghee or vanaspati 5 cups

To make 50-60 jangiri

Clean the rice and black gram dhal and soak together in 3-4 cups water for half an hour to 1 hour. Wash well. Grind into a paste. The paste should be somewhat rough. Take the rough paste, little by little, and grind once again till smooth, sprinkling a little water while grinding.

Mix the water and sugar. Heat to prepare syrup. When the syrup begins to boil, add the milk to remove the scum. When the syrup reaches thread consistency, add rose essence. Mix saffron. Remove from fire and keep aside.

Take a wide frying pan. Heat the ghee or vanaspati. Let it not smoke. Place a lump of the black gram dhal paste in a 'jilebi ret'. Keep the dough in the middle. Gather the ends and press the dough through the hole, holding the cloth over the fat. Make a complete circle. Make scallops in the anti-clockwise direction over the first circle. Then make another circle and end at the starting point itself. Make four to five such jangiris at a time. Cook till golden on both sides. Remove from fire.

Take the hot jangiris out of the fat and dip in warm syrup. Keep dipped in the syrup till the next batch is cooked. Before dipping the next batch in the syrup, take out the earlier batch on to a plate. Continue till all the dough is used up.

Note:

To prepare the 'jilebi ret', take a very thick square of cotton cloth. Make a small hole in the middle and stitch it, using the button-hole stitch.

The paste should not be kept for long. As soon as it is ground, it must be used immediately.

If the jangiris are not soaked in warm syrup while they are still hot, i.e., immediately after frying, they will not absorb the syrup, even if kept in the syrup for a long time.

If the syrup becomes thick while frying the jangiri, place the thickened syrup on the fire and add a little hot water to make it thin.

MYSORE PAK

Ingredients

Sugar 4½ cups
Water 2 cups
Ghee 4-4½ cups
Bengal gram flour 1½ cups

To make 40-50 pieces

Photograph on p. 100

Mix the water and sugar. Heat to prepare syrup. When the syrup attains a thread consistency, add 1 to 1½ cups of ghee.

Sift the Bengal gram flour, removing all the lumps. Sprinkle the flour little by little into the syrup while stirring continuously with a flat spoon. When the flour and syrup mix well, add the remaining ghee little by little, stirring all the while. Keep stirring till the preparation gives an appetising aroma and the Mysore pak froths up.

Pour it on to a plate greased with ghee and spread evenly by gently shaking the plate. Let it cool. When it is three-fourths cooled (i.e., when the ghee is absorbed and small holes appear on the surface), cut into convenient sized squares or diamonds with a greased knife. Remove the pieces from the plate and keep in an airtight container after cooling.

Note:
Use pure ghee only.

COCONUT BURFY

Break cashewnuts into bits. Fry in a little ghee till golden. Powder cardamom. Grate the coconut into soft, fine bits.

Mix water and sugar. Heat to prepare a thick syrup. Add grated coconut and stir. When coconut and sugar mix well and become hard, add fried cashewnuts and ghee, turning continuously with a flat spoon, till the mixture swells up. Mix in cardamom powder and continue to stir for a few more minutes. Remove from fire and pour on to a greased plate. Tap the surface evenly with a plantain leaf. Cut into square or diamond shaped pieces with a knife. Cool and keep in airtight containers.

Note:
The scum must be removed completely from the syrup while boiling. Otherwise, the burfy will not be milky white.

Ingredients

Cashewnuts 20
Ghee ¼ cup
Green cardamoms 7-8
Coconut 2 (Large)
Water 1 cup
Sugar 3½ cups

To make 40-50 pieces

Photograph on p. 100

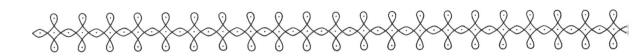

COCONUT SOJJI APPAM

Ingredients

Coconut 1 (Large)

Cashewnuts 12

Ghee or vanaspati 2 cups

Sugar 1 cup

Green cardamom powder 1/2 tbsp

Salt 1/4 tsp

Refined wheat flour (Maida) 2 cups

To make 20-25 appam

Grate coconut and grind nicely. Break cashewnuts into bits and fry in a little ghee till golden. Mix 1/5 cup water and sugar in a vessel. Heat to prepare a thick syrup. When the syrup attains a two thread consistency, add coconut paste and cook till the mixture turns smoothly leaving the sides. Add cardamom powder and fried cashewnuts. Mix well. Roll into small balls. Keep aside.

Mix the salt and refined wheat flour. Knead into a dough, with enough water and 5-6 tbsp ghee.

Grease a small bit of plantain leaf with ghee. Take a little dough and flatten out into a thin circular shape. Place a ball of the coconut 'fillings' in the centre, draw the edges together to completely cover it. Invert this on the plantain leaf. Flatten it out with your palms. The appams are now ready to be fried.

Heat the ghee or vanaspati over a slow fire. Fry the appams, cooking both sides. (Do not let the appams turn reddish.) Remove from fire. Drain out the oil and serve.

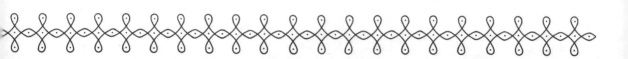

POLI

Grate coconut and grind nicely. Break cashewnuts into bits and fry in a little ghee till golden. Mix 1/5 cup water and sugar in a vessel. Heat to prepare a thick syrup. When the syrup attains a two thread consistency, add coconut paste and cook till the mixture turns smoothly leaving the sides. Add cardamom powder and fried cashewnuts. Mix well. Roll into small balls. Keep aside.

Mix the salt and refined wheat flour. Knead into a dough, with enough water and 5-6 tbsp ghee.

Heat a flat pan used for pancakes. Grease a plantain leaf with oil. Take a little of the dough and flatten it out to the size of your palm like a thick poori. Place a ball of the coconut 'fillings' in the centre, draw the edges together to completely cover it. Flatten it out again by pressing the filled dough twice with your hand. The edges can be rolled evenly with a rolling pin. Invert the flattened 'poli' with the leaf over the pan. Gently lift the leaf, leaving the 'poli' on the pan. Dribble 1/2 tsp of ghee round the 'poli' and another 1/2 tsp over it. Cook one side. Turn and cook the other side. Remove from pan and serve.

Note:
Jaggery may be used instead of sugar, if desired.

Ingredients

Coconut *1 (Large)*
Cashewnuts *12*
Ghee or vanaspati *2 cups*
Sugar *1 cup*
Green cardamom powder *1 tsp*
Salt *1/4 tsp*
Refined wheat flour *(Maida) 2 cups*

To make *10 poli*

THIRATTUPAL

(SWEETENED MILK KHOYA)

Ingredients

Full cream milk 4 litres
or
Ordinary milk 12 litres
Sugar 2-3 cups
Ghee 50 gms (Optional)
Green cardamom powder
½-1 tsp
Borneal flakes ¼ tsp
(Optional)

Take a heavy vessel. Pour the milk in it. Place on a low flame and heat well. Stir continuously as the milk heats and reduces in quantity. When it starts reducing, keep turning till the milk attains a semi-solid consistency. Add the sugar and stir again. Mix well till the milk thickens. If the 'thirattuppal' does not ooze fat, add the ghee and stir again. Remove from fire. Add cardamom powder and borneal flakes (if used).

While the 'thirattuppal' is being prepared, it will stick to the sides of the vessel often. Scrape the sides of the vessel with a ladle, otherwise the 'thirattuppal' will get a scorched smell. Cook on a low flame, even after the milk starts hardening.

COCONUT BALLS

(THENGAI KOZHUKATTAI)

Wash rice at least three times. Soak for 2 hours. Wash
again twice and drain. Spread the rice on a white cloth
and dry in the shade. Turn rice once or twice. Grind into
rice flour in a mill or mixie/food processor the next day.
Sift through a fine sieve. Alternatively, after washing the
rice, pound in a stone mortar with an iron pestle, sift
through a fine sieve and dry in the shade. The flour
should be completely dry to avoid lumps at the time of
using. In case the flour is not quite dry, or if the rice is
new, reduce the quantity of water to be used. Ready-
made rice flour can also be used.

Boil 3 1/2-4 cups water with salt and oil. Add the rice
flour. Keep turning with a spoon for about 5 minutes.
Do not allow lumps to form. Soak a white cloth in water
and rinse out. Spread it over a plate. Empty the hot,
cooked flour over the cloth. Tie the cloth into a bundle
and keep aside. (This will keep the flour free from
lumps.) When cold, untie the bundle and knead well.
Make it into three equal parts and keep covered with a
cloth. Take a little of the flour and knead well into
dough with a little water, if necessary. Grease your
palms with a little oil. Take a small lump of the kneaded
dough and shape it in your palms into a cup. Fill the
cup with the prepared filling and close all the sides well
to prepare the 'kozhukattai'. Make 'kozhukattais' with
all the dough and fillings.

Ingredients

Rice 2 cups
Salt 1 tsp
Gingelly oil 1 tsp

For the filling

Coconut 1 (Large)
Powdered jaggery or sugar
3/4 cup
Green cardamoms 6-10

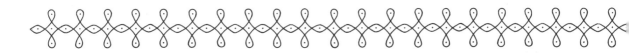

Place a single idli tray in a vessel with water in the
bottom. Cover the vessel and bring the water to boil.
Spread a white cloth over the tray and place a greased
plantain leaf over it. Arrange a few 'kozhukattais' on it.
Close the vessel and steam them over a high flame for
about 10 minutes till the 'kozhikattais' are cooked. Wait
till the steam condenses and drips out. This is an
indication that the 'kozhukattais' are cooked. (The colour
would have changed and they will not stick.) Open the
lid. Take the tray out and pull out the leaf with the
'kozhukattais' on to another plate. Sprinkle a little water
over the plate. Spread another greased leaf on the tray
and arrange a few more 'kozhukattais'. Steam as before.
Repeat till all the 'kozhukattais' are cooked.

For the filling: Grate the coconut finely. Add a little
water to the powdered jaggery and place on fire. Wait
till the jaggery melts and the water begins to boil. The
syrup will thicken and froth up, giving a nice aroma.
Add coconut gratings. Go on stirring over a slow fire.
Cook till water is fully absorbed and the filling becomes
sticky. Remove from fire. Powder the cardamom and
add. Cover the mixture and let it cool. If sugar has been
used, add a little water and boil till the syrup thickens
and froths up. Add coconut gratings. Go on turning till
the water is fully absorbed. Remove. Mix cardamom
powder. Keep covered and let it cool.

SWEET CHEEDAI

Wash and soak the rice for 3-4 hours. Dry the rice and powder in a mill or mixie/food processor. Sift the flour through a coarse sieve. Roast the sieved flour in a hot iron or earthen pan. When the flour can be drawn into a line (holding a small pinch of flour between the thumb and forefinger, draw a line with it on the counter), remove from fire. Sift once more, and ensure all the lumps are broken.

Add 1/4 cup water to the jaggery. Place on fire and prepare a thin syrup. When the syrup begins to smell appetising, drop a little into a cup of water and check consistency. The jaggery syrup should be soft enough to be rolled, but firm enough to float on the water. When the syrup is ready, remove from fire. Add the roasted and sieved flour. Mix well, turning well with a ladle.

Cut coconut into very fine bits. Dry roast black gram dhal and powder it to make a very smooth powder. Add the coconut, dhal powder, cardamom powder and gingelly seeds to the rice flour in the jaggery syrup. Knead into a smooth firm dough. Pinch and roll into small marble-sized balls and spread the 'cheedai' on a cloth. Do not smooth the surface of the balls too much.

Heat vanaspati, oil or ghee in a frying pan. Gently lower ten or twelve balls at a time into the oil and fry till a dark red colour, turning very gently. Drain and serve.

Ingredients

Rice 2 cups
Jaggery 2 cups
Coconut 1/2 (Medium)
Black gram dhal 1/4 cup
Green cardamom powder 1/2 tbsp
White gingelly seeds 1/4 cup
Vanaspati, ghee or coconut oil 1 1/2 -2 cups

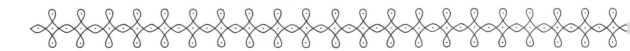

Note:

If excess jaggery is used or if the syrup is over-boiled, the 'cheedai' will break up into bits. If the jaggery is in excess, add 4 tsp pounded rice flour and knead.

The rice flour may be mixed with the jaggery syrup a day earlier. On the next day, crumble the rice flour-jaggery mix nicely, add black gram dhal flour, gingelly seeds and coconut bits and knead into a firm dough with enough hot water. If the rice flour-jaggery mix has hardened and does not leave the vessel, sprinkle a little hot water, heat slightly and pound it. Knead with the other ingredients and use.

The coconut may be added with the jaggery when making the syrup.

Salads, Pachadis & Chutneys

PLANTAIN STEM SALAD

((VAAZHAI THANDU KOSUMALLI)

Remove the fibre from the plantain stem. Wash the plantain well. Cut into four lengthwise pieces and then into thin slices, or into fine bits. Soak the pieces in a mixture of water and buttermilk with 1 tsp salt and the turmeric powder. Mix well and let it stand for half an hour. Squeeze out the water and keep in a bowl.

Cut the lime in halves. Dip both halves in the remaining salt. Squeeze the lime with the salt into the vegetable. Pinch the curry leaves and add to the cut vegetables. Flavour with the asafoetida water. Heat the oil in a pan. Fry the mustard and slit green chillies. When the mustard splutters, add to the salad to season it.

Ingredients

Plantain stem 1/2 kg
Water 3/4 cup
Buttermilk 3/4 cup
Salt 1 1/2 tsp
Turmeric powder 1/4-1/2 tsp
Lime 1 (Medium)
Asafoetida water 1/2-1 tsp
Curry leaves (Broken) 2 tbsp
Oil 2 tsp
Mustard seeds 1/2 tsp
Green chillies 2

To serve 4 persons

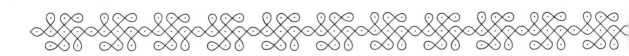

CUCUMBER SALAD

(VELLARIKKAI KOSUMALLI)

Ingredients

Cucumber 1 (Large) or 2 (Small)
Lime 1 (Medium)
Black peppercorns ½ tsp
Cumin seeds ¾ tsp
Salt 1 tsp
Oil 2 tsp
Mustard seeds ½ tsp

To serve 4 persons

Scrape the skin off the cucumbers if they are of the big variety. Small, tender cucumbers can be used with the skin. Slice the cucumber. Extract lime juice. Coarsely powder the pepper, cumin and salt. Mix with the cucumber slices. Heat the oil and add the mustard. When it splutters, remove from fire and add to the cucumber slices. Add lime juice and mix well.

BENGAL GRAM DHAL SALAD

(KADALAI PARUPPU KOSUMALLI)

Soak the dhal for a few minutes in water. Drain and wash the dhal thoroughly. Cook the dhal in 1 cup water. Do not overcook the dhal. The dhal can also be cooked in a pressure cooker. Extract lime juice.

Heat oil in a frying pan. Add the mustard and slit green chillies. Add cooked dhal, salt, asafoetida water, curry leaves and grated coconut. Stir for a few minutes. Remove from fire and mix the lime juice before serving.

Ingredients

Bengal gram dhal 1 cup
Lime 1 (Medium)
Oil 2-3 tsp
Mustard seeds ¾ tsp
Green chillies 2-3
Salt 1 tsp
Asafoetida water ½-1 tsp
Curry leaves (Broken) 2 tbsp
Coconut (Grated) ¼ cup

To serve 4 persons

MANGO PACHADI

(MAANGA PACHADI)

Ingredients

Mango 1 *(Medium)*

Water 3/4 *cup*

Salt 1/2 *tsp*

Turmeric powder 1/4 *tsp*

Jaggery 100 *gms*

Rice flour 2 *tsp*

Oil 2 *tsp*

Mustard seeds 1 *tsp*

Green chillies 2

To serve 4 *persons*

Do not peel the mango. Cut it into big bits. If the skin is too thick, scrape it lightly.

Heat the water. Add mango bits, salt and turmeric powder and cook. When the mango is cooked, add the jaggery. Let it mix well. Mix rice flour in water and add. Boil for a few minutes (till everything mixes well). Remove from fire. Heat oil. Fry mustard and green chillies and season the 'pachadi'.

Note:

The mango should neither be too tender nor too ripe. It must be both sweet and sour.

Green chillies may be cooked with the mango instead of being used as seasoning.

If green chillies are not available, fry two dry red chillies with the mustard and season.

Ripe or half-matured mangoes may also be used. Remember to adjust the quantity of jaggery suitably.

JACKFRUIT PACHADI

(PALAPPAZHAM PACHADI)

Remove the fibres from the sections. Cut the sections into small bits. Heat the water. Add salt and turmeric powder to the water and cook the cut fruit in it. When the jackfruit is cooked, add the jaggery. (You may reduce or increase the amount of jaggery depending on how sweet the jackfruit being used is.) Mix well. Mix rice flour in water and add. Boil for a few minutes (till everything mixes well). Remove from fire. Heat oil. Fry mustard and green chillies and season the 'pachadi'.

Ingredients

Jackfruit (Sections) *1 cup*
Water 3/4 cups
Salt 1/2 tsp
Turmeric powder A pinch
Jaggery 100 gms
Rice flour 2 tsp
Oil 2 tsp
Mustard seeds 1 tsp
Green chillies 2

To serve 4 persons

Note:

Fully matured or partially matured jackfruit may be used. If the fruit is of very good variety, the pith (the portion remaining after taking the fruit sections and discarding the thorny skin) can also be used.

TENDER MANGO PACHADI
(MAVADU PACHADI)

Ingredients

Tender mangoes 7-8
Green chillies 4
Fresh curd 1 cup
Salt ½ tsp
Oil 1 tbsp
Mustard seeds 2 tsp
Coriander leaves (Chopped) 3 tbsp

To serve 4 persons

Wash the mangoes in water and soak in hot water (the water should be just enough to cover the mangoes) till soft. Drain water. Grind the mangoes with one green chilli. Mix the ground mangoes with curd and salt. Heat oil in a frying pan. Fry the mustard and remaining green chillies. Season the curd. Garnish with coriander leaves and serve.

Note:

Sometimes, tender mango pickle turns too soft. These mangoes can be used to prepare the 'pachadi' as well. Remember to wash the mangoes and reduce the quantity of salt and chillies as the pickle itself contains both.

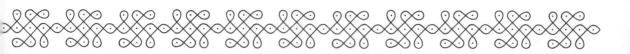

LADY'S FINGER PACHADI

(VENDAKKAI PACHADI)

Use tender vegetables to make this dish. Cut the lady's fingers into thin round slices. Heat 5 tsp of oil and fry the cut lady's finger. Mix salt in the curd. Heat remaining oil and fry mustard and green chillies. Add the seasoning and fried vegetable to the curd just before serving. Mix well and serve.

The vegetable may also be cut into small bits and fried in 2 to 3 tsp oil with the cut green chillies and 1/4 tsp salt and added to the curd on cooling. Season with mustard.

Ingredients

Lady's finger 100 gms

Oil 6-7 tsp

Salt 1/4 tsp

Curd 1 cup

Mustard seeds 1 tsp

Green chillies 2

To serve 4 persons

Photograph on p. 117

LADY'S FINGER TAMARIND PACHADI
(VENDAKKAI PULI PACHADI)

Ingredients

Lady's finger *175 gms*

Green chillies *5-6*

Tamarind *A lump the size of a lime*

Oil *6 tsp*

Salt *1¼ tsp*

Jaggery *One marble-sized lump*

Rice flour *2 tsp*

Fenugreek seeds *½ tsp*

Asafoetida powder *A pinch or to taste*

Mustard seeds *1 tsp*

Curry leaves *(Broken) ½ tsp*

To serve *4 persons*

Use tender lady's fingers for this dish. Cut the lady's fingers into thin rings. Chop green chillies. Soak the tamarind in water and prepare a fairly thick juice. Heat 4 tsp oil. Add the vegetables and green chillies and fry well. Add the tamarind juice and salt to the vegetable. Boil well. Add the jaggery. Mix rice flour in water and mix with the 'pachadi' after the jaggery melts. Boil. Dry roast the fenugreek seeds and asafoetida powder. Mix with the 'pachadi' when still boiling. Remove from fire. Heat 2 tsp oil. Add mustard and when it splutters, season the 'pachadi'. Garnish with curry leaves.

COCONUT PASTE

(THENGAI THUVAIYAL)

Grate the coconut. Heat oil. Fry all the ingredients, except the coconut and salt, to a reddish colour. Grind tamarind, salt, fried red chillies and fried asafoetida to a smooth paste, adding a little water. Add coconut gratings and grind into 'chutney'. (The paste should be very smooth.) Add fried mustard and fried black gram dhal and grind lightly again. Now the chutney-like paste is ready for serving.

Note:

For any 'thuvaiyal', the quantity of salt, chillies and tamarind must be adjusted to taste. If you increase the quantity of salt and chillies, remember to increase the quantity of tamarind as well. Quantities of rest of the ingredients may be kept the same.

Ingredients

Coconut 1 *(Medium)*

Oil 4-5 *tsp*

Tamarind A lump the size of a lime

Salt 2 *tsp*

Dry red chillies 7-8

Asafoetida A pinch or to taste

Mustard seeds 1 *tsp*

Black gram dhal 3 *tsp*

To serve 4 *persons*

ONION PASTE
(VENGAYA THUVAIYAL)

Ingredients

Onion *350 gms*
Oil *7 tsp*
Dry red chillies *10-12*
Mustard seeds *1 tsp*
Black gram dhal *3 tsp*
Asafoetida *A pinch or to taste*
Tamarind *A lump the size
of a lime*
Salt *2½ tsp*

To serve *4 persons*

Peel onions and slice. Heat 2-3 tsp of oil in a frying pan and fry the sliced onions. Keep aside. In the same frying pan, heat 4 tsp of oil. Fry separately the chillies, mustard, black gram dhal and asafoetida to a reddish colour. Grind the fried chillies, asafoetida, tamarind and salt. Add the onion and grind further. Add fried mustard and dhal. Grind once or twice. Mix well and serve.

Note:

For any 'thuvaiyal', the quantity of salt, chillies and tamarind must be adjusted to taste. If you increase the quantity of salt and chillies, remember to increase the quantity of tamarind as well. Quantities of rest of the ingredients may be kept the same.

COCONUT CHUTNEY

(FOR DOSAIS AND IDLIS)

Squeeze the juice from the lime. Keep aside. Grate the coconut. Keep aside. Heat 1 tsp oil. Fry 4 tsp Bengal gram dhal. Remove from fire. Grind the grated coconut with salt, green chillies and the fried dhal. Heat the remaining oil in a frying pan. Add mustard and 1 tsp Bengal gram dhal. Season the chutney. Add the asafoetida water and lime juice for flavour and mix well.

Note:
A marble-sized lump of new tamarind may be substituted for the lime.

Instead of frying the Bengal gram dhal, it can be soaked raw and ground with the coconut.

Popped Bengal gram dhal ('pori kadalai') may be used in place of Bengal gram dhal.

Ingredients

Lime 1 *(Medium)*
Coconut ½ *(Medium)*
Oil 2 *tsp*
Bengal gram dhal 5 *tsp*
Salt 1¼ *tsp*
Green chillies 7-8
Mustard seeds ½ *tsp*
Asafoetida water 1 *tsp*

To serve 4 *persons*

Photograph on p. 118

PICKLES

SPICY LIME PICKLE

(YELUMCHANGAI KARA URUGAI)

Choose juicy limes to prepare this pickle.

Heat 2-3 cups of water in a heavy vessel. When the water begins to boil, put the limes in it. The water must cover the limes. Bring to boil. Add turmeric powder. Remove from fire and keep tightly covered. When cool, cut the limes into small pieces. Mix in the salt. Sprinkle chilli powder on top.

Heat oil in a frying pan. Put mustard in it. When it splutters, pour the hot oil (making a circular motion) over the chilli powder. Roast the fenugreek seeds to a dark red colour in a frying pan. Fry the asafoetida in 1/2 tsp oil. Powder the fenugreek and asafoetida together. Mix well into the pickle. Fill a bottle with the pickle and keep tightly corked.

Note:
If chilli powder is not available, lightly fry about 100 gms of red chillies. Roast 1 tsp fenugreek seeds. Fry 2-3 tsp asafoetida. Powder these together with salt into a smooth powder. Mix with the cooked and cut lime. Season with 1 tsp mustard fried in 1/4 cup of gingelly oil. Mix well and store.

Ingredients

Lime 6
Turmeric powder 1/4 tsp
Salt 1/4 cup
Chilli powder 6 tsp
Gingelly oil 1/4 cup
Mustard seeds 1 tsp
Fenugreek seeds 1 tsp
Asafoetida A pinch or to taste

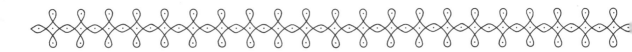

TAMARIND CHILLI PICKLE
(PULI MILAGHAI URUGAI)

Ingredients

Tender green chillies 100 gms

Tamarind A lump the size of a big lime

Fenugreek seeds ½ tbsp

Gingelly oil ¼ cup

Asafoetida A pinch or to taste

Mustard seeds 1 tsp

Turmeric powder ¼ tsp

Salt ¼ cup

Jaggery A lump the size of a marble

Slightly slit the green chillies (on the narrow side). Keep aside.

Soak tamarind in water and prepare juice, adding 3/4 cup water, a little at a time. Filter and keep aside.

Heat a heavy vessel and roast the fenugreek seeds in it till they turn a dark reddish colour. Keep aside. Heat the oil in the same vessel and fry the asafoetida. Keep aside. Powder the fenugreek seeds and asafoetida together into a smooth powder. In the same oil, add the mustard. When it splutters, add the slit chillies and turmeric powder. Fry well. Add tamarind juice and salt and boil. Add the fenugreek and asafoetida powder to the boiling liquid. Add the jaggery. Boil till it mixes well and the mixture becomes thick and semi solid.

MAVADU

(SPICY TENDER MANGO PICKLE)

Tiny little tender mangoes, pickled whole, make a
favourite side dish for South Indians. The first crop of
little baby mangoes ('mavadu') as they appear on the
trees are taken and pickled. There are also special kind of
trees that yield mangoes, which are suitable only for this.
Mountain varieties are the best suited for this pickle.

Wash the mangoes well in a lot of water. Empty into a
bamboo basket or sieve to drain off water completely.
Grind mustard and turmeric into a smooth paste.
Spread mangoes on a tray and smear the mustard-
turmeric paste and castor oil evenly over the mangoes.
Clean and wipe dry a porcelain jar. Put in a handful of
salt. Add 4 handfuls of the smeared mangoes. Add salt
and chilli powder. Repeat layers of mangoes, salt and
chilli powder for all the mangoes. Close the lid. After
two days, mix well by giving a good shake to the jar.
Cover the top of the pickles with a layer of remaining
salt and chilli powder. Allow to stand for at least 2
weeks before using.

Alternatively, finely powder the red chillies and salt
together. Grind the mustard and turmeric into a paste.
Mix the paste with the castor oil. Put into the jar. Put the
mangoes over it and finally add the chilli-salt powder
and mix well.

You can also boil 8 cups (2 litres) of salt with 8 cups
(2 litres) of water, till the salt dissolves completely and

Ingredients

For Mountain Varieties

Tender mangoes 48 *cups*
Mustard seeds 2 *tsp*
Turmeric root 3 *(each piece
3"-4" long)*
Castor oil 3 *tsp*
Salt 8 *cups*
Dry red chillies 8 *cups*
or
Chilli powder 2 *cups*

*For Ordinary (Garden)
Varieties*

Tender mangoes 64 *cups*
Mustard seeds 4 *tsp*
Turmeric root 3 *(each piece
3"-4" long)*
Castor oil 4 *tsp*
Salt 8 *cups*
Dry red chillies 8 *cups*
or
Chilli powder 2 *cups*

Photograph on p. 135

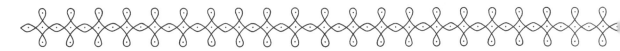

the water is reduced to half its volume. Remove from fire and cool well. Grind the mustard and turmeric together into a paste. Pour 1/3 cup of the salt water into the jar, the mustard-turmeric paste, a little chilli powder and a portion of the mangoes (in the order mentioned), repeating the layers till all the salt water, chilli powder and the paste are used up. This helps the mango retain its colour for a long time and prevents it from getting soft and spoilt.

Note:

Remove the stalks from the mangoes. However, do not pinch out the stalk completely. Leave about 1/2 inch of stalk on every mango.

Do not powder the chillies in a mill, but pound it at home with a pestle. This will help the mango 'stay' longer. The chillies may also be powdered in a mixie/food processor.

AVAKKAI

(SPICY MANGO PICKLE)

Select a very sour and fibrous variety of mango for this pickle. Wash and completely dry a porcelain jar.

Wash the mangoes well. Wipe dry, using a cloth.
Cut the mangoes lengthwise into two halves, including the seed inside. Then, cut it into small bits (about twelve to sixteen bits) taking care to keep the seed in the bits also. Spread the bits on a tray and dry in the sun for about 1-2 hours. Remove when the mango bits have dried completely. Take a wide, galvanised vessel or a tray. Place all the other dry ingredients in the tray, add the oil and prepare a smooth paste. Take a few mango bits at a time, mix them well in the paste, and put them in the jar.

Mix three-fourths of the bits like this, and mix the other quarter, all together, in the paste, and put it in the jar. Cover the mouth of the jar with a clean white cloth. Tie the cloth tightly around the mouth and keep the jar aside. Open it on the third day, and turn the pickles well, from bottom to top with a spoon. Thereafter, every day, turn the pickles well once a day, and cover again tightly. The pickles will be ready in 8-10 days.

Take a few mango bits and keep them in a separate small jar for your day-to-day use. If the bits are too big, cut them again into smaller bits and serve. It is very important that the jar should always be kept well

Ingredients

Mango 25 (*Medium*)
Chilli powder 4 *cups*
Salt 4 *cups*
Mustard powder 2 *cups*
Turmeric powder 1 *cup*
Fenugreek seeds ¼ *cup*
Bengal gram (*whole*) 100 *gms*
(*Optional*)
Gingelly oil 4 *cups*

covered, with the cloth tied tightly. This pickle will keep for more than a year, if stored properly.

Note:

For this pickle, it is desirable to use oil pressed from white gingelly seeds. If this oil is not available, use ordinary refined oil.

As some people may not like the smell of mustard powder, modify the quantity of mustard, according to taste. Since a lot of mustard is used, there is no need for asafoetida. However, one moderately big lump of asafoetida may be added, if desired.

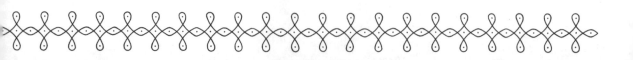

MANGO THOKKU

Large and sour mangoes with hard, ripened seeds should be used for this recipe.

Peel the mangoes. Grate or chop the mangoes into small bits. Heat a heavy vessel. Roast the fenugreek seeds till they turn black. Remove and keep aside. Heat 2 tsp of oil and fry the asafoetida. Keep aside. When cool, finely powder the fenugreek and asafoetida together.

Heat the rest of the oil in the same vessel. Add mustard and allow to splutter. Add the mango, turmeric powder and salt. Stir the mixture well. When the mango has cooked, mix in the chilli powder and stir seven or eight times. (The mango has cooked when the water let out from the cooking mango has evaporated and the mixture forms a ball and leaves the sides of the vessel.) Mix in the prepared fenugreek and asafoetida powder. Remove from fire. Cool and bottle.

In place of chilli powder, fry 2 cups of red chillies lightly in oil. Roast the fenugreek seeds and fry the asafoetida. Powder all these three together with salt. Heat the remaining oil. Add the mustard and allow to splutter. Add the mango and turmeric powder. Fry well till all the water has evaporated and the mango has cooked. Mix in the powdered chilli, fenugreek and asafoetida. Keep on fire for some time more. Keep turning till everything mixes well. Remove from fire. Cool and bottle.

Ingredients

Mango *4 (Large) or 6 (Medium)*
Fenugreek seeds *1 tsp*
Gingelly oil *1/2-3/4 cup*
Asafoetida *A marble-sized bit*
Mustard seeds *2 tsp*
Turmeric powder *1/2 tsp*
Salt *1/2 cup*
Chilli powder *1/3 cup*

Note:

Adjust the quantity of salt and chilli powder according to the size and sourness of the mango.

If the mango cannot be grated or chopped to bits, peel the skin off the mangoes. Cut into large bits and grind with salt into a pulp. Then proceed as above.

For pickles and 'thokkus', a small quantity of white asafoetida (also known as 'milk asafoetida') can be used along with the ordinary asafoetida.

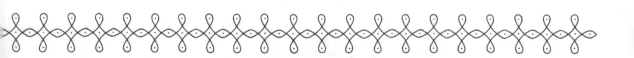

LIME THOKKU

Cut the lime into small bits. Remove the seeds. Mix with the salt and turmeric powder. Keep it covered for a day. On the next day grind the lime into a nice paste in a stone mortar or mixie/food processor. Keep a heavy vessel, e.g., white stone vessel ('kalchatti') on the fire and pour a little oil into it. Fry the asafoetida. Powder it and keep aside. Fry the mustard in the same oil. After it splutters, add the lime paste and go on turning, till it is cooked and forms a ball. Take care that it does not stick to the sides. Add the chilli and asafoetida powders. Mix well and remove from fire. Store in a bottle.

If there is no chilli powder, fry 1/2 cup dry red chillies and asafoetida in oil. Powder them together, adding half the salt. Add the other half of the salt to the lime and keep it for two days. Fry the mustard and the lime pulp, and cook. When cooked, remove from fire, add the chilli-salt-asafoetida powder. Mix well and store in a bottle.

Ingredients

Lime 6 *(Large)*
Salt 35 *gms*
Turmeric powder 1/4 *tsp*
Oil 1/4 -1/2 *cup*
Asafoetida A *pinch or to taste*
Mustard seeds 1 *tsp*
Chilli powder 6 *tsp*

Veppilai Katti

Ingredients

Lime, lemon or citron leaves
8 cups
Salt *¼ cup*
Dry red chillies *10-15*
Asafoetida *A pinch or to taste*
Thyme seeds *2 tsp*

This pickle is prepared with lime, lemon or citron leaves. They may be used separately or mixed. A non-oily pickle, it can be used as a side dish with curd rice.

Select good leaves without insects. Take out the mid ribs. Powder all the ingredients together, preferably in a clean dry stone mortar with an iron pestle or in a mixie/food processor. Prepare as fine a powder as you can. Store the powder in an airtight container.

Note:

Curry leaves may also be prepared in the same way, after removing the stalks. The leaves should not be very ripe.

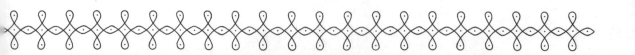

MISCELLANEOUS

SAMBAR POWDER

Dry the red chillies in the sun for one day. Powder it in a mill. Separately dry the coriander seeds, pepper, turmeric, Bengal gram dhal and red gram dhal in the sun for a day. Powder these together in a mill or mixie/food processor. Mix with the chilli powder. Store in an airtight container. For daily use, store a little powder separately in a smaller airtight container. This way the powder will remain fresh.

Ingredients

Dry red chillies 350 gms
Coriander seeds 350 gms
Black peppercorns 3 1/2 tbsp
Turmeric root 7-8 (each piece 2"-3" long)
Bengal gram dhal 1/2 cup
Red gram dhal 1 cup

RASAM POWDER

Dry coriander seeds, red gram dhal and pepper in the sun for a day. Powder coriander seeds separately, as smoothly as possible. Sift and keep aside. Powder red gram dhal and keep aside. Fry red chillies in the oil for 2 to 3 minutes. Powder the fried chillies as smoothly as possible. Mix the coriander powder, the red gram dhal and pepper powder and the chilli powder together. Optionally, turmeric root can be ground with the coriander seeds to give a good colour to rasam.

Ingredients

Coriander seeds 3 cups
Red gram dhal 1/2 cup
Black peppercorns 1/2 cup
Dry red chillies 8 cups
Turmeric root 20 pieces (Optional)
Oil 4-6 tsp

CHILLI POWDER

(FOR DOSAI)

Ingredients

Gingelly seeds ¼ cup

Gingelly oil ⅜ cup

Black gram dhal ¼ cup

Bengal gram dhal ¼ cup

Dry red chillies 3 cups

Coconut (Ripe) ½ (Medium)

Asafoetida powder A pinch
or to taste

Salt ½-¾ cup

New tamarind A lump the size
of a lime

Jaggery 2-3 tsp

Mustard seeds 1 tsp
(Optional)

Dry roast the gingelly seeds in a frying pan till they splutter and pop. Heat oil. Fry the dhals in the oil separately, one after the other, to a reddish colour. Pinch out the stalk from the chillies and fry till crisp. (Do not allow it to turn black.) Grate the coconut and fry to a reddish colour. Fry asafoetida.

Powder the gingelly seeds first. Add salt and tamarind. Powder well. Add the fried red chillies, coconut and asafoetida next and powder. Finally add the jaggery and fried dhals and powder till the dhals are broken. Mix well and bottle.

Note:

Take care to remove the seeds and fibres from the tamarind.

This powder may also be prepared without coconut and tamarind. The quantity of gingelly seeds may be increased, if desired.

Coconut, tamarind and gingelly seeds may all be omitted as well. Instead, fry the red chillies, asafoetida, mustard, Bengal gram dhal and black gram dhal. Powder them together with salt to prepare the powder.

Powdering the ingredients with a pestle is preferable to powdering them in a mixie/food processor, as the former method gives the powder a better taste.

FILTER COFFEE

You will need a coffee filter for this. Steel coffee filters of various sizes are commonly available.

Boil 2 cups of water. Put the coffee powder in the upper compartment of the filter. Place the perforated disc over that. Pour the boiling water on the disc. The coffee decoction will drip into the lower compartment of the filter. Pour out the filtered decoction into a vessel. Boil the remaining 1/2 cup of water and again pour this into the filter. If necessary, mix the second decoction with the first to prepare 2 cups of decoction.

Boil the milk, stirring it two to three times. Remove from fire. Keep 1/3 cup of the milk aside. Mix the rest of the milk with the decoction. If milk is not enough, add the milk set aside. Mix sugar to taste. Dissolve, stirring with the spoon. The coffee is ready to be served. Pour the coffee into individual mugs/steel tumblers from a height to get the froth.

Ingredients

Filter coffee powder 8 tsp
Water 2½ cups
Milk 2 cups
Sugar 4 tsp

To serve 4 persons

Photograph on p. 136

NOTES

1 cup measure is equivalent to 250 ml.

1 tsp = 5 ml

1 tbsp = 3 tsp

A pinch = less than $1/8$ tsp (literally a pinch)

Unless otherwise stated, use refined oil for all recipes.

To prepare asafoetida water, take the quantity of asafoetida, add a little water and mix well. Wait till the lump dissolves in the water. The quantity of asafoetida water so prepared would depend on the size of the lump.

To pinch curry leaves, crush them lightly in your hand before adding.

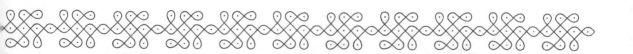

GLOSSARY

Almond	*Badam Paruppu*	Cinnamon	*Sanna Lavangapattai*
Amaranth Stem	*Keerai Thandu*	Cloves	*Kirambhu*
Anise Seeds	*Soambhu (Perum*	Cluster Beans	*Kothavarakkai*
	Jeerakam)	Coconut	*Thengai*
Arecanut	*Kottai Pakku*	Colocasia	*Seppangkizhangu*
Ash Gourd	*Pooshanikkai*	Copra	*Kopparai Thengai*
Baking Soda	*Soda Uppu*	Coriander Leaves	*Kothamalli*
Banana	*Vazhai Puzhum*	Coriander Seeds	*Kothamalli Vidhai*
Bangalore Brinjal	*Chow-chow*	Country Sugar	*Nattu Sarkarai*
Beaten Rice Flakes	*Aval*	Cucumber	*Kakkarikkai, Vellarikkai*
Bengal Gram Dhal	*Kadalai Paruppu*	Curd	*Thayir*
Bengal Gram Flour	*Kadalai Mavu*	Curry Leaves	*Kariveppilai*
Betel Leaves	*Vetrilai*	Dates	*Perichampazham*
Betel Nut	*Paakku*	Drumstick	*Murungaikkai*
Bhir Fruit	*Ilandai Pazham*	Dry Ginger	*Sukku*
Bitter Gourd	*Pavakkai*	Elephant Yam	*Chenai Kizhangu*
Black Gram (Whole)	*Ulundhu*	Fenugreek Seeds	*Vendhayam*
Black Gram Dhal	*Ulutham Paruppu*	Garlic	*Poondu*
Black Gram Powder	*Ulutham Mavu*	Ghee	*Nhei*
Boiled Rice	*Puzhungal Arisi*	Gingelly Oil	*Nallennai*
Borneal Flakes	*Pachaikarpooram*	Gingelly Seeds	*Ellu*
Bottle Gourd	*Suraikkai*	Ginger	*Inji*
Brinjal	*Kathirikai*	Green Gram Dhal	*Paasi Paruppu*
Broken Beans	*Mochai Paruppu*		*(Payatham Paruppu)*
Butter	*Vennai*	Gooseberry	*Nellikkai*
Buttermilk	*Moar*	Grapes	*Drakshai Pazham*
Cabbage	*Muttakose*	Greens	*Keerai*
Camphor	*Choodam*	Green Chillies	*Pachai Milaghai*
Capsicum	*Kudamilakkai*	Green Peas	*Pachai Pattani*
Cardamom	*Elakkai*	Groundnut	*Verkadalai*
Cashewnut	*Mundhiri Paruppu*	Groundnut Oil	*Kadalai Ennai*
Castor Oil	*Vilakkennai*	Guava	*Goyya Pazham*

Honey	*Thane*	Radish	*Mullangi*
Incense Stick	*Oodhu Bathi*	Raisin	*Drakshai (Ularndha)*
Jackfruit	*Palappazham*	Red Chillies	*Milaghai Vatral*
Jaggery	*Vellam*	Red Gram Dhal	*Thuvaram Paruppu*
Kerosene	*Mann Ennai*	Refined Oil	*Suddhikarikapatta Ennai*
Lady's Finger	*Vendakkai*	Ribbed Gourd	*Peerkankai*
Lentil Beans	*Kaaramani (Thattai Paruppu)*	Rice	*Arisi*
		Rice Flour	*Arisi Mavu*
Lime	*Yelumchangai*	Roasted Bengal Gram Dhal	*Porikadali*
Mango	*Maanga*		
Mango (Ripe)	*Mampazham*	Sabre Beans	*Avaraikkai*
Mavadu	*Tender Mango*	Saffron	*Kumkumappoo*
Milk	*Paal*	Sago	*Javvarisi*
Mustard	*Kadugu*	Salt	*Uppu*
Neem Flower	*Veppam Poo*	Semolina	*Rava*
Nutmeg	*Jatjikkai*	Snake Gourd	*Pudalankai*
Onion	*Vengayam*	Sugar	*Sakarai*
Paddy	*Nell*	Sugar Candy	*Karkandu*
Par-boiled Rice	*Puzhungal Arisi*	Sweet Potato	*Sakaraivallikizhangu*
Pepper	*Molagu*	Tamarind	*Puli*
Pineapple	*Annasi*	Tomato	*Thakkali*
Pistachio	*Pistha Paruppu*	Thyme Seeds	*Omam*
Plantain	*Vazhaikkai*	Turmeric	*Manjal*
Plantain Flower	*Vazhaippoo*	Turmeric Root	*Varali Manjal*
Plantain Stem	*Vazhai Thandu*	Vermicelli	*Semia*
Pomegranate	*Mathulam Pazham*	Vitis	*Pirandai*
Poppy Seeds	*Kasa Kasa*	Wheat	*Godhumai*
Potato	*Orulaikizhangu*	Wheat Flour	*Godhumai Mavu*
Pumpkin	*Pooshnikai*	Wood Apple	*Vilampazham*
Pumple-moses	*Paplimas*	Yam	*Senai*